BELIEVE EG21

PLAY LIKE THERE IS NO TOMORROW

Mike McCann

Believe EG21: Play Like There Is No Tomorrow
© 2015 Michael Edward McCann

Grateful acknowledgement is made to the following for permission to reprint previously published material:

"Prosperity in Afflictions" (pages 190, 191) devotional by Os Hillman: Reprinted by permission from the author. Os Hillman is an international speaker and author of 15 books on workplace calling. To learn more, visit http://www.MarketplaceLeaders.org

"CSU football team and Coach Jay Mills" Image (page 71): Used with permission from the Charleston, SC Post and Courier.

Charleston Southern vs. Coastal Carolina images (pages 210, 222, 232): Used with permission from Willis Glassgow and the Big South Conference.

ISBN 978-0-9966905-1-5

Published by Mike McCann

To my family and coaches, whom I thank for believing in me.

To my teammates, to whom I'm forever bonded.

To Ed and Paula, who raised an amazing son. May he live forever in our hearts and the pages of this book.

TABLE OF CONTENTS

"The uniform makes for brotherhood, since when universally adopted it covers up all differences of class and country."
– Robert Baden-Powell

CHAPTER 01

HUMBLE BEGINNINGS

SUNDAY, DECEMBER 15, 2002

JACKSONVILLE, FL

Jay Mills dropped to his knees on the floor of a dingy hotel room in Jacksonville, Florida with tears welling up in his eyes. He faced the floral print of the full size mattress and clasped his shaking hands against his forehead. "Lord, I can't do this, too much needs to happen. If I'd have known how bad the program was, I wouldn't have taken the job. Please... If this is where you want me, please show me how to handle this."

Mills had recently been chosen as the new head coach for the Charleston Southern University football team in North Charleston, South Carolina, but he was not ready for the challenges that awaited him. As he sat in the hotel room, defeated, he ran through the laundry list of issues to address: a plan for recruiting players didn't exist, nor did money to recruit, the locker room needed major improvements, video equipment was needed to record practices and games, administrative help was missing, and the coaches didn't even have cell phones. It had been 11 grueling years since CSU played its first-ever home game sanctioned by the National Collegiate

Athletic Association, college athletics governing body commonly referred to as the NCAA, after six years of club ball. After 17 years the program didn't seem to have money for anything.

Mills was on the road recruiting players in Northeast Florida when he felt the swelling pressure to give up. As a man of God, Mills finally sought strength from the only place he knew could restore his faith. He opened his Bible and what started as a moment of weakness, turned into a revelation. The pages seemed to flip themselves to Proverbs 16:3. *"Commit to the Lord whatever you do, and your plans will succeed."*

Stunned, but not surprised that The Lord chose to speak to him in such a way, Mills sat in silence and reflected on the scripture and his situation. As fast as the excuses piled up, the solutions started forming in his head. It wouldn't be easy, but it would be possible. In his mind and in his heart, Coach Mills knew this is what he'd always wanted: to earn the honor and responsibility few deserved as the head coach of a Division 1 football team.

As Coach Mills left Jacksonville on his way home to Charleston, South Carolina, he was rewarded for his faith. He stopped in Beaufort, South Carolina at the home of a baby-faced, curly haired high school quarterback. The player had been offered by Mills' predecessor, but had yet to make a decision. The player's older brother was on the basketball team at Charleston Southern University so the young man was already familiar with the program. Unsure if that familiarity was good or bad, he pulled up ready for the worst but praying for the best. Collin Drafts could be the biggest recruit the school landed in 2003 if everything went well. He was smart, a key component for Mills' complex offense. He was also an accurate passer and could make plays with his legs if needed. Mills' plan was to sit Collin on the sideline as a freshman while redshirting him. The redshirt year, very common for freshman football players who aren't ready to play, would postpone the start of his eligibility for one season. He could learn the offense from the comfort of the sideline, get accustomed to college life, and strengthen his body during the "rebuilding" seasons Mills knew were unavoidable. With a couple years of grooming, Collin could be a major threat in the Big South. He was highly recruited throughout the state, but had yet to make a decision. Mills, only having been on the scene for a handful of days, had limited communication with the Drafts family. He had no idea what to expect.

His palms were sweating and the weight of the program pressed on him like a vice.

KNOCK KNOCK KNOCK

The door flung open with enthusiasm he wasn't quite ready for.

"You must be Coach Mills! Come on in, it's so nice to finally meet you!" He was greeted by a full smile and a sweater that read "C-S-U" in navy blue lettering – both of which belonged to Collin's Mother, Pam Drafts. Mills breathed a small sigh of relief. He knew he had a quarterback for the future.

Collin committing to CSU was a blessing, but Coach Mills knew he had many other positions to recruit. He needed offensive linemen in the worst way. Plus, he had to find a number of receivers to make his no-huddle system function. His next stop was Atlanta to scout a young man named Nick Ellis who could serve two roles, freeing up an additional scholarship. Reminded once again that every dollar and every scholarship counted in his tight budget, having one young man that could kick field goals, perform kickoffs, and punt would be another blessing for his program.

Ellis's name came from a Harvard recruiting list Coach Mills used the year prior. Mills' time as the offensive coordinator for the Crimson earned him the reputation that helped him land the head coaching job at CSU. Ellis was a scholarly player at Union Grove High School in the suburb of McDonough, Georgia with a GPA above 4.0. He was respectful and mature for his age. Although Nick was "only a kicker," he had a passion for winning that rivaled any defensive lineman or running back Mills had ever seen.

After meeting with Ellis, Mills was thoroughly impressed and offered him a scholarship on the spot. Ellis jumped at the chance to join the growing team.

As many tactful head high school coaches tend to do, coach Scott Mason wanted to share all the other "Division 1" athletes his school had to offer now that he knew Mills had scholarships to give. Mason's intentions were pure, but Mills knew most of the players weren't Division 1 athletes. If they were, he'd already know their names. Plus, he had to get back to Charleston to figure out this whole "no-money-anywhere" problem. He had time to look at one more player while he was at Union Grove so he asked to see the best player that had not been signed.

After turning down a full scholarship to a Division 2 school, the player eventually signed as a walk-on for the 2003 Charleston Southern University Football recruiting class. He was prepared to sacrifice whatever was necessary to become a full scholarship Division 1 athlete. He was a wide receiver named Edward "Eddie" Gadson.

— — —

Coach Jay Mills inherited a program lacking a full roster of scholarships, a recruiting database, or even decals for the helmets. But the school supported him. The athletic department made some tough decisions and cut the men's soccer program leading up to Mills' first season so football could have 10 additional scholarships. Mills, who held an accounting degree, had extensive experience in the finance arena. He used this knowledge to organize Pell Grants and academic scholarships that would bring the football team much closer to a full roster of scholarship athletes beginning with the 2003 season.

The school's leadership also approved his request for a $100,000 recruiting budget after demonstrating the program's need to attract competitive players comparable to those on other teams in the Big South Conference. This budget was approved on the grounds he would recruit players who could walk on, not just scholarship players. Since he needed as many bodies as he could get, this was a no-brainer.

The only problem: CSU was a private school and out-of-state tuition wasn't exactly cheap. As most smaller schools do, Mills started recruiting his local turf for the best players that wanted to play Division 1 college football. He scoured the state in search of talent comparable to Collin Drafts. He found some local players like Jada Ross from the storied Summerville High program, who had been passed over by a number of Division 1 schools, but he had minimal success.

Charleston Southern already had a reputation in the minds of the high school coaches in South Carolina. The reputation could be summed up in one phrase the CSU coaches had to hear more than once on recruiting visits: "Haha, are you serious?"

The Bucs' reputation wasn't that of an established program. More established schools, such as Wofford College, would easily attract players based on their academic and athletic traditions. Other schools, like Coastal Carolina, had the advantage of brand new facilities earning them the label of "a program on the rise." Many of the high school coaches flat out refused to let Coach Mills and his newly assembled staff talk to their Division 1 players. Ultimately, the coaching staff was forced to recruit out of state. As a result, many of the players from in-state were walk-ons because Coach Mills refused to compromise. Bringing Division 2 players into a Division 1 program to be put on full scholarship was unacceptable.

Mills also knew if he recruited only high school players he would have to wait three years for the team to mature into experienced juniors or redshirted sophomores. Something Mills did not want to wait around for.

Always thinking ahead, Mills heavily recruited junior college players who could immediately contribute. From his days at Harvard, he knew many of the JUCO's, as the junior colleges were referred to, on the East Coast were filled with players who had academic issues. Even if Mills found and signed talented players, they may never become academically eligible to compete. Since many of them may not be accepted to CSU, he decided not to waste his limited resources on the East Coast junior colleges and went straight to the Golden State.

California JUCO's, unlike many on the East Coast and in the Midwest, were filled with players who simply couldn't play at the few large schools on the West Coast. California was overcrowded with talented football players – they didn't have academic issues and they were talented enough to play Division 1 football. A recruiter's dream. The abundance of players caused many talented young men to slip through the cracks. Coach Mills capitalized on this talent and brought waves of Californians and other West Coasters into the program during his first formative years of the program.

Soon the discipline for which Mills became known began to set in. In his first season he would set the foundation for winning games. Even if that foundation cost him players and wins, he wouldn't compromise. If players had disciplinary issues, they were gone. Some on their own terms, some on Mills'.

Mills wanted to redshirt as many players as possible in 2003, allowing them to grow and develop while watching from the sidelines. He wanted to avoid wasting players' eligibility because he knew the team's best chances of winning games wouldn't happen for another year. Losses would be inevitable. But if he could save players' eligibility for the coming years, the sacrifice would be justified. He knew his best team wouldn't be present in 2003 and he sacrificed games knowing the best was yet to come.

Mills would do anything to keep from burning players' redshirts. At one point in the season, he had to literally pull a man from the stands, give him a helmet and shoulder pads, and put him on the field to play in the second half. During another game in 2003, the roster had only 35 active players when a normal Saturday sideline includes roughly 60 players, all of whom can step on to the field and participate. To say the 2003 team struggled is an understatement.

In present day, our Charleston Southern University football team has become a family of 90 brothers from all over the country. We have diverse backgrounds and all of us have unique "legends" about what got us to CSU. One thing is constant: we would do anything for each other. We were not one of those teams that bickered and one-upped each other. We didn't have scuffles outside of the practice field with each other. We had a team mentality; nobody was out for themselves. We had a strong bond and we were set on doing something amazing with our time at Charleston Southern University. This is our story.

CHAPTER 02

COMPETITION

WEDNESDAY, FEBRUARY 16, 2005

NORTH CHARLESTON, SC

"IN! Just inside the line, it counts!"

"Come on man, you didn't make that and you know it! How could you see if you made it in? You're all the way back there!" Eddie was ticked. Toning down his competitive side was simply not an option.

The guy he was arguing with wasn't backing down either. "Yeah right! In! You can still see the marks on the ground. It's plain as day!" Someone from the sideline was shouting for the other team. Their fan section was larger than ours and it was increasingly apparent we weren't going to win this argument.

"Don't worry about it, we're pounding them anyways, it's only one point. Let's get it back right here!" I tried to distract him but the expression on Eddie's face told me I was failing miserably.

Growing up a coach's son I was unintentionally, or maybe not, groomed to remain level headed throughout competition. The shadow my dad's football career cast was something I was eager to escape from, but the lessons he shared about the game were priceless. I didn't get as worked up as Eddie, but I wasn't about to let them score any more cheap points. I was glad Coach Mills landed that Eddie Gadson kid from Atlanta. He made me want to win. And, he was an awesome volleyball player.

"Apparently Backwards Hat over there is the official ref!" Eddie huffed, referring to the player he'd just argued with, saying it just loud enough for Backwards Hat and everyone on the sand court to hear.

"Four serving 18. Let's get it back this time!" Nick Ellis chimed in with me, sensing Eddie's frustration at our lack of total dominance. Nick had gone to high school with Eddie and knew better than to argue with him about something like this; it was pointless. The unseasonably warm afternoon allowed us to shed our winter clothes for the impromptu volleyball game. Eddie's shoulders tightened under his sweaty wife beater, his hands gripped his thighs, his eyes narrowed onto Backwards Hat. He shook his head as he crouched into his defensive position, pulling his shorts just above his knees.

"Yeah but they shouldn't have won that point. That didn't land in. We earned it!" Eddie grumbled.

At that point I realized just how competitive Eddie Gadson was. Those years of basketball, golf, and volleyball alongside his dad on Air Force bases around the world had built up this winning attitude with a broken off-switch. Most of us, including the other team, couldn't care less about one point. Eddie played the point like his scholarship depended on it. Before the ball crossed the net on next serve, Eddie sprung into the air and spiked the ball into the sand. He dove for one-handed saves and relentlessly finished points. He inspired my roommate, CJ Hirschman, Nick, and me to crank up our level of play. Soon, I was covered in a mixture of sweat and sand from running, diving, and jumping all over the court.

Backwards Hat and his squad remained scoreless the rest of the match. We pummeled his crew of co-eds for two more games before heading back to the dorms to clean up for dinner. The Quads, as the dorms were affectionately known, got their name from their square architecture and housed most of the football team along with other regular students. The Southern Baptist values of the school strictly forbade coed dorms; guys only at the Quads.

It didn't matter what we were doing, we were always around each other. Practice and workouts consumed most of our time, but we found each other during classes and sat next to each other at meals. Extracurricular activities, although they were few and far between with our busy schedules, were no different.

Nick and Eddie were fun to hang out with, but CJ and I were inseparable. We lived together, we both played in the defensive secondary, we hung out together on the weekends, and we even took the same business classes. We often sat up late night talking about how much trouble we caused in our shared hometown of Jacksonville, Florida. We schemed ways to graduate early and work the school system during lunch. But more than anything, we talked about how to win more football games.

As CJ, Nick, Eddie, and I walked back to the Quads, our conversation drifted from class to girls to home and, inevitably landed on football.

"I've never lost five games in my career, 2004 was the most frustrating season of my life," CJ was still disappointed about our performance from the previous year. He played cornerback last season and earned playing time, but that wasn't where he wanted to be, nor was it his strength. He was currently making a case to the defensive backs coach, Darrell Perkins, that he should play safety next season. Given his seemingly mystical powers of charm, I wouldn't be surprised if he got his wish.

"Yeah, but it was way better than 2003... that was brutal. Y'all are lucky you weren't here then," said Nick. He and Eddie were a year older than CJ and me, though Nick seemed like an enlightened older man. Maybe the cool confidence was something he developed from all those years kicking field goals under pressure. "Compared to our first year, 2004 was a major accomplishment."

"I'm with CJ. I came from a big program in high school," I added. "We shouldn't be satisfied with five and five. And only one conference win shouldn't cut it, we were so close in the last two games. We're another year older and we've got a ton more experience under our belts." As a true freshman, I was fortunate enough to play in every game but one during the 2004 season. By the last game of the season, I was playing a whole new game. It's amazing the difference a year of experience makes.

"Nobody said we were satisfied," Eddie chimed in with some leftover intensity from the volleyball court. The primadonna wide receiver mold didn't fit Eddie Gadson. "But it's improved over the year before, like Nick said. And we gotta keep working if we want this year to be better. We didn't work as hard as I thought we could have leading up to last season. This year, we're all doing 5:30 a.m. workouts and spring ball together. We'll be light years ahead of where we were last year. But we have to make it happen right now, in the off-season."

We all agreed without reservation. Most of the spring semester is a relaxing time for us, especially in the afternoons. 5:30 a.m. workouts, not so much... After a 5-5 season we all knew we had to get better. These afternoons in the Charleston sun were fun, but 12 hours away was a world of pain ready to smack us in the face.

I didn't mind the work. I never had a chance; my fate as a football player was set before I was born. I grew up in a family full of athletes and coaches. I had always aspired to live up to the legend of Coach McCann, my dad. Growing up I was told tales about his days at the University of Florida and since birth I had been donning the Gator orange and blue. He coached or employed many of my high school coaches and I couldn't go anywhere in our tight-knit beach community without someone asking me, "McCann, eh? So, are you Billy or Mike's kid?" My family thought I would follow in Dad's footsteps at the University of Florida. Florida was an option – if I wanted to walk on and pay for school. When CSU and other schools began offering me scholarships I knew I could never turn down the opportunity. Although Dad would have loved it if I tramped the same tracks as a Gator, he was proud that I earned a full ride and fulfilled my own dream.

Dad wasn't the only athlete. Mom, a personal trainer by trade, held four years of college tennis under her belt and encouraged physical activity at every turn. She instilled in me a work ethic and influenced my faith. Before I left for school she lost hours of sleep worrying about me. She knew I had a solid foundation, but I was fiercely independent and I moved out from under both parents' roofs before I had earned my high school diploma. She thought she had done a subpar job raising me. I tried to convince her that she did such a fantastic job and I was just ready to leave the nest early. She loved that CSU had recruited me. She relished in the fact that I could attend school in a Christian environment and that Coach Mills was a man of faith. She encouraged me to go to a college where they cared about "me as a man, not just as a player."

For all these reasons and some I didn't entirely understand, I chose CSU because I fit the program and it fit me. "Home" was now Charleston Southern University. My family from the beach was still there for me, but I had adopted 90 other brothers and a handful of "uncles" over the past year.

"See ya tomorrow fellas," Nick said as CJ and I parted toward our room.

I retorted with a smirk, "Bright and early!"

CHAPTER 03

5:30 A.M. WORKOUTS

THURSDAY, FEBRUARY 17, 2005

NORTH CHARLESTON, SC

BEEEEP

"Switch!"

We sprinted to the corner of the gym to the unrolled wrestling mat as fast as we could, all vying for the front of the line. Coach Steve Barrows wore a mischievous grin as we raced toward him. The linebackers coach seemed to enjoy torturing us through the mat drills. He fancied himself a player's coach. His playful personality made him relatable and his midnight blue, also known as "purple" to us, Honda Shadow motorcycle gave him some street cred – in his own mind if nowhere else.

"Sprint fellas! Get your butts in gear!" he said with his whistle hanging out of his mouth like an unlit cigarette. "First group, get ready! Up-down! Left! Seat roll left! Seat roll right! Up-down!" Coach Barrows' hands flashed back and forth with precision.

"Win the drill. Gotta move faster. Gotta push." My mind raced almost as fast as my feet.

"Feet! Feet! Feet!" He always looked funny when he was putting on his best serious face. Especially when he flushed red from all the screaming.

"Right! Seat roll right!"

Too winded to laugh. Gotta focus.

"Buzz em! Buzz em! Sprint past me! Next group!"

Each Tuesday and Thursday morning at 5:30 a.m. we conditioned for an hour and a half. The workout consisted of six stations comprised of various agility, speed, and stamina exercises that replicated football movements and tested our will. We were broken into small groups and rotated around the echoing gym until we had completed all six stations. Four minutes of excruciating work at each stop. At the end of the sixth station, you'd be hard pressed to find a dry article of clothing in the gym.

Barrows' mat drills were miserable, but the worst was still to come. Rotating through the six stations in the gym provided ample tenderization for conditioning: gassers. Gassers consisted of timed trips across the width of the basketball court. We'd start with 16 trips back and forth without stopping; 60 seconds to complete the round. Then we halved the trips and the time until we reached two trips with six seconds. If the coaches were satisfied with our performance, we wrapped for the morning. If not, we continued to work back up the ladder. Mills would never let us know exactly how many were left, knowing someone would try to work the system or "save some" for later.

If you didn't make your times you earned extra conditioning after the workout. The entire team was present so failing in front of 77 other guys was unacceptable. Most opted to puke before they'd miss their times, a regular occurrence during gassers.

I thought I knew how to work hard, but I learned how to push myself to another level during those sweaty mornings under the buzzing fluorescent gym lights. The body will do exactly what the mind instructs it to do. If your mind gives in, your body follows suit. If your mind is ready to keep going, your body will find a way. The coaches challenged us and teammates encouraged each other, but ultimately it came down to each of us as individuals. We had to figure out how much we were willing to suffer, how much pain we were willing to endure to win those drills. The ones willing to push the hardest could be found at the front of the pack.

BEEEEP

"Switch!"

Gassers were a long way away though. Coach Barrows' mat drills were only our second stop on the tour de gymnasium. "Group one, break it down and get your butts out of here!" Coach B was out of breath and was starting to sweat through his gray sweatshirt that read "BUCCANEER FOOTBALL" on the front.

After eight months around the coaching staff the whole no-cursing-but-keep-up-the-intensity thing still took some getting used to. Most of the time I wanted them to be tougher on us. But not right now. My mind raced faster than my legs on the sprint to the next station. "Gotta be first, gotta set the tone."

"Group two, let's go! You know the drill, pro shuttle, get a partner. McCann and Misher start us off!" Coach Darrell Perkins, our defensive backs position coach who wasn't much for nonsense, didn't have to say much. He spoke simply with a sort of non-stop breathing like he was exhaling when he spoke. He coached simply, no need for elaborate schemes if we can't play the basic ones first. He even wore a simple hair cut, his light brown skin completely shaved above the shoulders other than his minimalist eyebrows. When he noticed a handful of the DB's comprising our group, he let us take charge. "First pair up, GO!"

If you were 30 seconds late to workouts you ran. If this was your second strike your position group ran. Heaven help you if it was your third strike. The entire team had to run all because you couldn't get out of bed on time. We were learning teamwork and accountability pretty early in the day. Especially when punishment runs came just as early on Saturday mornings, our day off. I was first in every drill and I was never late. My teammates had a nice way of reminding me how I had a tendency to make them keep up.

"Come on Mish, we got a long way to go. It's only group three. Stand tall." My encouragement was falling on deaf ears. He beat me in the pro shuttle, but I wouldn't let him slouch. I scanned the group, doing my best to stand instead of slump, and looked for individuals to encourage. "Come on fellas, stand up!" I said with more force and a few claps to emphasize my point. That got their attention. David Misher gave me a snarl as he moved his hands from his knees to clasping over his head and slowly filed back in line. I knew he'd blast me at the breakfast table. I didn't care. Deep down I know he didn't either. Somebody had to push us. I decided a long time ago it would be me.

"Push, fellas! Push, fellas! Faster! Faster!" I could see David encouraging the others out of the corner of my eye. I knew he'd come around.

BEEEEP

"Switch!"

I was coming into my sophomore year and I wanted to compete with the best of the best. I wouldn't be outworked by anyone. I had to beat Eddie Gadson. If I beat him, everything else would seem like cake. Eddie, the hardest working guy on the team, never took a play off, not even during 5:30 a.m. workouts. If I could keep up with him, I could earn a name for myself. This competition was natural during the season since he was a receiver and I was a defensive back, but I carried it over to off-season training. He was my barometer during these early mornings.

Eddie stood 5'9" on a "tall" day. His jet black hair complimented light brown skin and he owned just enough facial hair to grow a pencil-thin mustache. His legs were so bowed they resembled the silhouette of a football, coming together only at opposing ends. When he smiled, the corners of his eyes drew tight and the dark brown of his iris was all you could see. His crooked smile, though absent in this moment, was contagious.

He straddled the line between cocky and confident. He thrived on competition and he hated, more than anything in the world, to lose. It didn't matter if he was walking 18 holes with his dad, volleyball with coeds, or trying to beat his teammates in gassers. Eddie wanted to win every single time.

Although Eddie only played in three games during his first year, 2003, he earned a scholarship for a breakout game against our intrastate rival, Presbyterian. He was forced to take a medical redshirt for a broken bone in his face and he couldn't finish the season, but he impacted the small returning squad.

He was snubbed by every Division 1 school in the country. He attended three high schools in four years, some of which were overseas with his parents. His senior year at Union Grove wasn't enough exposure to attract attention from larger programs. He received offers from some smaller schools and even turned down a full ride to one of them because he knew he could earn a scholarship at CSU if he was given the chance.

He knew he was Division 1 material. He knew he was good and he played with a chip on his shoulder. He had a loud, cocky persona on the field, but a calm confidence in the locker room when he spoke to you one on one. He ran a sub-par 40 yard dash, but he caught everything that came within his grasp. And he outworked everyone.

In his single year at Union Grove High School, Eddie occasionally found himself between groups of friends. He could listen to country music with the white kids from the farm and he could play basketball with the black kids from the city. Though his teachers saw him fit in with ease, his closest friends knew that sometimes he felt like an outsider to all parties. His parents raised him without prejudice and he saw everyone the same, though the treatment wasn't always returned. As many of us were in high school, "Okinawa Eddie" felt like he was somewhere in limbo. He found the opposite to be true in college. His mixed complexion allowed him to connect with, or challenge, everyone equally. Here at CSU, color didn't matter. Work ethic, ability and attitude were how we were judged. Three characteristics that Eddie personified.

Eddie brought in 69 catches in his redshirt freshman year in 2004. But he, like the rest of us, wasn't satisfied with those numbers or our record. So here we were, pushing each other to get better.

Eddie and I knelt side by side in a three-point-stance, ready to sprint through an L-drill. From the starting cone we'd sprint five yards ahead, then back, then ahead once again before taking a hard turn in opposite directions for five more yards and sprinting back to the starting point via the "L" shape. If he wins, I do push-ups. If I win, he does push-ups.

Under his Blue Jersey his standard issue yellow t-shirt was covered in sweat, as was everyone else's in the gym. His navy blue shorts labeled "CSU" seemed too big for his frame. They hung low around his knees as we sunk down into our stances.

"GO!" shouted Coach Chris Achuff, the new defensive line coach. He had only been with us for a matter of days and his intensity still took some getting used to. We talked it over and all agreed; Coach Achuff was borderline insane, but we needed a couple coaches like that to keep us motivated.

If you showed leadership by finishing every drill with enthusiasm, pushing your teammates, and working your butt off, you had a chance at a Blue Jersey. 'Blue Chip' jerseys were given to the top tier guys who worked harder than anyone on the team. Sixty other college athletes were hard to beat. Eddie had been Blue Chip since day one. I found out why as he smoked me in the shuttle. He looked back as we jogged to the back of the line, "Hey McCann, get yo weight up!"

On the outside I laughed, you couldn't go five minutes

without hearing that phrase around here. On the inside, I was fuming. Eddie wasn't the only competitive person on the team. We came back and stood side by side in identical, hands locked on our heads, stances. We'd occasionally unlock them to applaud for our teammates as they repeated the drill we just finished. I tried to wipe the sweat from my face, but couldn't find a dry spot on my clothes.

"Good work, bro, keep it up." He almost whispered the encouragement while I dropped down into a pushup position. Just loud enough for me to hear, but not loud enough for anyone else to take notice. Eddie could only keep up the taunting so long. He was a leader and he wanted to win, but he didn't want to demoralize anyone on his side.

BEEEEP

"Switch!"

"Here we go! Break it down fellas! Great work Blue Chips!" His scream pierced our ears. Coach Achuff was sweating almost as much as us, though he wasn't running. "Sprint to station five! Keep it moving!"

We had been assigned groups when the session started. Each of us had been rated by the coaching staff on our individual performances at the previous workout with a number, one through six. Your average score from the last session determined which group you'd be placed in the next session. Overall, there were six groups to match the six stations through which we rotated. All the Blue Jerseys were in group one. Now that I made it to this elite group, I knew I had to step up my game.

"What are you lookin' at me for? You know what we're doing! One foot in each bag, GO!" the last word exploded from Coach Kelly's mouth. Chuck Kelly, the offensive line coach, wasn't up for pleasantries. He needed a few more Diet Cokes before he could relate to us. The good news: bag drills were our last station. The bad news: bag drills were still work.

"No rest. Gotta sprint. Get through fast. Keep working. Set the tone." I was even out of breathe in my own mind. Keeping this Blue Jersey was a ton of work.

I was constantly trying to match the work Eddie put in. But, it seemed like he just didn't get tired. He was a machine or something! I could beat him once, maybe twice, but never three times. He was consistent and persistent and he never let anyone see him hurt. During practice he never let the defense see when we got to him. Our starting middle linebacker, known for vicious hits, baptized Eddie with a tackle so hard that his neck landed on the ground before his body. Before we knew it he bounced back up like it never happened, jawed at the defender and the rest of us on defense for a bit on his way back to the huddle, and never once showed the pain. I found out in the locker room after practice that he was so shook up from the hit he couldn't go in for two plays. We never knew; he never showed it. Guess that's why he always earned a Blue Jersey.

BEEEEP

"Get some water and start walking laps!" Coach Mills voice was a relief from the bag drills. "Gassers will start in four minutes and 50 – 49 – 48…" Well, a momentary relief at least.

I was ready to collapse. I glanced at Mish, he looked as tired as me. I gave him a nod, no need to waste energy with words right now. We gave each other a quick low five. I scanned the gym for the rest of my competition. CJ Hirschman was drenched. Starting cornerback Marvin McHellon was winded. Josh Mitchell, our middle linebacker and my other roommate, concentrated on looking tough. He wasn't fooling anyone.

Though seven months away, this is where we earned our wins. We sacrificed today because we wanted to celebrate in the fall. We were willing to trade the pain of gassers for the pain of losing.

The coaches set up the trash cans near the ends of the gym, no need to get vomit on the clean gym floors. Not only did gassers teach us to push ourselves, they taught us to compete. More than any other station, this is where Blue Jerseys were won or lost. If I could be at the head of the pack, I'd lock down a Blue Jersey.

I knew I was in for a long morning when I looked over and saw an obnoxious grin on Eddie's face. He was just getting started.

CHAPTER 04

INDOOR PRACTICE

TUESDAY, APRIL 5, 2005

NORTH CHARLESTON, SC

We had legitimate reason to dream; we improved significantly over the past semester. We worked harder than ever during 5:30 a.m. conditioning and competition flooded spring practice worse than the thunderstorms that graced campus each afternoon ever could. Spring ball, though finishing in four days, was filled with optimism and hope. We talked about the upcoming season, our opponents, and, on occasion, let ourselves dream of a shot at a conference championship.

"Were any of y'all here at last year's spring game?" I asked everyone behind me.

As defensive backs, our warm-ups consisted of ball drills. We'd take off toward Coach Perkins after he'd signal us with a ball tap, adjusting to the ball wherever he threw it. Although they could be physically demanding, we were rarely serious. As we approached this year's spring game, I couldn't help but make fun of last year's.

"I was," giggled Jon Carmon, our most outspoken cornerback, "It was pathetic! They only had like 30 guys on the field!" He rarely passed up an opportunity to make fun of someone. Jon came in with me as a freshman the previous year. He quickly became known for running his mouth more than his legs. He had slightly bowed legs and he looked too thick to be a cornerback. His round face seemed to be permanently printed with a smile, a mostly mischievous one. Jon was having fun today; he just officially earned the starting corner position.

"Good catch Marvin!" someone shouted.

"Bingo!" Marvin McHellon said to indicate his catch.

"Yeah, it was pretty bad. I came with my Mom and sister to the game," CJ was all smiles too. He'd talked his way into a position switch for him and Marvin. CJ would start at safety and Marvin would start at corner. This way, as CJ argued, they could both be on the field at the same time.

"Oh, we remember, CJ. We all remember who you were with," Jon quickly reminded him that we all noticed his family. Mom-jokes swirled and we all had a laugh at the expense of CJ. Jon could tell we were entertained and kept pushing. Soon he had every one of us laughing underneath our helmets.

"Oh yeah, CJ, we remember!" I yelled as I took off at an angle. Low and to the right. Got it. "Bingo!"

"Mike what are you talkin' about?" said Jon. "You had your shirt off way up there in the blue VIP seats like you were getting a tan or something!" I was an easy target for Jon and I rarely put up a fight, mostly because everything he said was true.

"That sounds about right. I'm not a fan of shirts, you guys know that. I didn't want to get a farmer's tan, plus I had to do something to keep myself entertained cause the game sure wasn't gonna do that." I peaked over to the oldest members of the secondary to see their reaction as I jogged back to the line.

We were a young secondary, but we had a few guys who had been around. Tavares Shorter, though widely looked up to, didn't talk much. He just huffed through his mouthpiece, shaking his head and adjusting his gloves. Tavares, a senior, had been one of the few consistent players for CSU over the past two seasons since transferring from JUCO.

Marvin agreed, and added, "But this year's gonna be much better. Isn't that right?" he locked eyes on me and, without words, gestured for a low five.

"You know it, Marv!" I reached down low and met his hand with mine. He smacked my helmet as if to say, "Let's move on from that, please," with the authority of an older brother teaching me a lesson. He knew how to keep focused when we got too high on ourselves.

I had grown immense respect for Marvin. He was the starting safety in 2004 and strove to be the hardest working player on the field. He never let us loaf and he always had a positive attitude. Even now as he changed positions, he was humble. He took on the new challenge with enthusiasm and not a peep of discontent.

"Let's get it!" hollered Coach Perkins from a distance, "Time to stretch!"

Today was going to be intense. We'd start practice with a drill called "3-on-3" immediately after warm-ups. The coaches would often start practice with a physical drill to prime us for the day's action. Nothing picked up the tempo or our attitudes like a big collision. Sometimes they surprised us so we didn't get too comfortable. Today, we saw it coming a mile away. All we could do was brace ourselves for it.

3-on-3 was comprised of eight players, four on offense and four on defense. Three offensive players lined up to block three defensive players, separated by about a foot of grass. If the offense sends out offensive linemen, we'll respond with our own "Big" players on the defensive line. If they send out their "Big Skill" or "Skill" players, we match up according to size on defense.

Five yards behind each line is a single skill player. They can be a sacrificial lamb or they can be the hero depending on who wants it more. The deep offensive man is typically a running back who is handed the ball as soon as the whistle blows. The defensive man is typically a defensive back being held on to by the back of the jersey. Like a rabid dog chained to a wall while a cat teases him, the defensive back is held until Coach Perkins decides it's "fair" we are let loose on the ball carrier.

Our version of "fair" often conflicted with Coach Perk's.

Sometimes the men up front can slow the ball carrier down or make the tackle. Other times it's a wide open shot, the defensive back and the running back go one on one in a space smaller than a doorway. No room for timidity, only controlled violence. If you hesitated, even for a split second, you were done. The running back would launch himself at you like a rhinoceros charging an attacker, making you look like a coward in front of your entire team. You'd be the laughing stock of practice for the rest of the day.

Marvin wasn't one to back down and he was up to represent us first in the back slot. The linebackers were first on the front line matched up against two tight ends and a fullback. They lined up facemask to facemask, so close they could smell each other's breath. The team circled up as close as possible, getting ready for the street brawl that was about to take place in front of our eyes. Nobody wants to miss the action. The screams and cheers grew louder as the front line settled into their stances. Marvin was calm and focused, as usual, ready to stick his nose into the fight.

Coach Kelly silenced us with a hand in the air, signaling the first snap.

BEEP BEEP BEEP BEEP

The weakest whistle in history told us something was wrong. A chorus of "aaawwww" rang out from everyone in a helmet.

"Men, we're headed inside, a thunderstorm is less than two

miles away. We're headed to the Brewer Center. On the hop!"
Coach Mills was almost as upset as us.

If you've ever lived in the South, anywhere near the coast,
you know what spring rainstorms are like. A typical day starts as
sticky as honey that just popped out of the microwave. By noon the
temperature feels like 100 degrees. Wind does nothing to relieve
the swelter, just swirl it around like a fan without air conditioning.
When stepping outside for more than 17 seconds a towel and a
change of clothes are necessary. The same steady, pulsating heat is
unrelenting until the sun goes down.

Thunderstorms, as punctual as Jay Mills himself, arrived
between three and four nearly every afternoon. To my native
Californian teammates, thunderstorms were a thing of wonder.
They didn't get lightning and thunder like we did out on the East
Coast and some were enamored by it. It was common to find guys
sitting out underneath the second story overhang watching the heat
lightning crack in the distance from a chair they drug out of their
dorm room in the evenings.

During the day, thunderstorms sounded like linebackers
during "train wreck" drill. They would come in fast, create
pandemonium, and leave a trail of destruction in their path. The
storms came fast, dumped loads of heavy rain on us and cracked
lightning all around our heads for 20 minutes. Then, with the
speed of a hurry-up offense, they'd vanish as fast as they appeared.
Leaving us with a heavy, pounding sun and muggy air.

One of these thunderstorms had crept up on us and forced
us into the gymnasium for the afternoon. Funds were tight at a
private institution like CSU so indoor practice facilities were but a
flicker in Coach Mills' dreams. The women's volleyball team had
already claimed the basketball court so we had to kick out anyone
in the intramural basketball gym and slop around in wet socks for
"walk-throughs." After we exchanged our cleats for shoes, we were
directed across the parking lot, past the tennis courts, and into the
back door of the tiny intramural gym.

As we walked in, we were met with glares from the students we'd just kicked off the court. Though the basketball court was regulation size, the gym felt like a dorm room meant for two stuffed with 10 people.

We went from a live tackling drill in our full gear to gingerly slopping around on a wet gym floor. This was not the practice we needed to have today. It took us 10 minutes just to get inside and organized. Tempers flared as the coaches snapped to get us focused. Some days I didn't know who was more competitive, the guys with the helmets or the guys with the whistles. We complied and started walking through our responsibilities in various sets.

As we faked a catch or mimicked a tackle, the coaches would remind us to "stay focused" and "work on your mental reps."

A taste of freedom came pouring through the back door as the athletic trainers checked their beeper-like devices for rain with the door cracked. Barely seven minutes into walking through our schemes, the rain was gone and the sun was beating down on the practice field across the parking lot.

"Back outside! Period six starts in three minutes!" shouted Coach Mills as we shuffled out the door toward the practice field. Our feet quickly transitioned from slipping on the gym floor to click-clacking on the asphalt of the parking lot. The steam rose through the thick, humid air and dragonflies danced in swarms to welcome us back to the practice field.

"Welcome to the South," I heard someone murmur from somewhere behind me. The native Californians had a way of continually comparing their homeland's supremacy to South Carolina.

We acted upset that we had to go back onto the field, but in reality we knew what we had to do. Spending our days in the gym wasn't the way to win games. With rules set in place by the NCAA, we were only allowed to practice for so many hours each week. We didn't love the idea of going out there again to the soaking wet field in wet gear, but we had no choice. We couldn't waste a valuable opportunity to get better.

The team that practiced in spring was largely the team that would compete in the fall. A few newcomers would contribute, though we didn't know who or how. If you went through the rigors of spring ball and the torture of 5:30 a.m. workouts, there are few reasons to abandon your team in the fall. Unless, it was not by choice.

CHAPTER 05

SUMMERTIME PASSING

SATURDAY, JUNE 18, 2005

NEPTUNE BEACH, FL

When the spring semester ended we all had choices to make. The coaches wanted us to stay and workout all summer like most larger programs did. I bought into that message the year prior with a grand total of nine guys who showed up for workouts. Four of them were forced to because of their grades, three more lived in the area year-round, and the other two were my roommate and me, as incoming freshmen. I thought the summer before was miserable, disorganized, and a waste of money since I had to pay out of pocket for my classes.

This summer, I decided to go back to work at the Neptune Beach lifeguard station back home in Jacksonville instead of working out with the team. Up to this point, my workouts were going well and I was getting paid to get a tan. I loved summertime. I'd talk with my teammates and I'd get to see CJ every few weeks since he was from the other side of Jacksonville.

On a blistering June day, Ryan "Reggie" Robertson called

me out of the blue. Reggie was a receiver which created a playful competition between us, as all receivers and DB's had. When I saw his Raleigh area code calling, I couldn't help but brighten up.

"Regg!" I shouted as I tossed the basketball haphazardly at the makeshift hoop on the deck of the lifeguard station.

"Hey buddy," he said with a somber tone.

"Hey man, how are ya? You back home in Burlington? What's up?" I was determined to cheer him up.

"Nah bo, I'm not doing that well. I guess that means you don't know, do you?" he asked, sounding more deflated than the basketball I was shooting.

"Uh, no I don't... What's up buddy? Everything OK?"

My questions went unanswered for what seemed like an hour. I walked from the front porch where we had been playing H-O-R-S-E to the back and sat down. Wiping the sweat from my face, I braced myself for whatever was about to come next.

On the other end of the line Reggie wiped his nose and cleared his throat. He had been crying, "Eddie died yesterday, Mike."

After a pause that seemed like an eternity, I blurted out the first things that came to mind, "What? How? What happened? Eddie Gadson, Eddie?" I pressed the phone closer to my head and blocked the noise of the basketball game with my opposite hand.

I couldn't hear anything except Reggie's voice. He was calm, but his voice was shaky. I hollowed as I listened to what had transpired. "He was back home, you know, outside of Atlanta. He was in a car accident... He was driving... too close... collision.... alone..." His short sentences were like knives piercing my chest.

Through the phone I could hear Reggie wiping the snot from his nose. I sat back in shock on the lawn chair I had confiscated for the conversation. I stared at the ground, I didn't have words.

"Reggie, I can't believe this... This is crazy... Wow...."

"Me too, man, I'm still in shock. He was one of my best friends on the team, and he's gone just like that. We were gonna room together this year..."

"I know he was, buddy, I'm so sorry. I am beside myself right now, that could have been any of us."

"I know, right? We've done much dumber things than just driving at night and nothing has ever happened to us. Life is short man."

"This is surreal... Do they have a date for the funeral yet?"

"Not exactly but it will be next week. Can you go?"

"Yes, of course, I'll be there, me and CJ can drive up from here to Atlanta. It's only five hours. Or fly or something, but we'll be there." CJ had a tough persona, but I knew he wouldn't hesitate to drop everything and make this trip. Like me, CJ put the team above nearly everything else in his life.

"OK, I'll be there, too. I'm going to meet up with Okeba and Edsel on my way through Charlotte. I know Collin is gonna drive up with his dad and Darius from Beaufort. As soon as I know an exact date I'll let you know."

"OK."

We held another long pause. "Alright bud, I have to make a few more phone calls but I'll talk to you later."

"Do you need me to call anyone?" Our phone tree system, though flawed, was the only way to communicate.

"Just CJ. Besides that, I think I've got it covered. Thanks, though."

"OK, will do. Love ya, buddy."

"Love you too, man. I'll call you when I find out about the arrangements."

A brotherhood exists within a team many outsiders would find hard to fathom. We push our bodies to the limits and then we push each other past them. We give all we can, and then we give more for the guys next to us. When it comes time, we are there to comfort each other through family tragedies, girlfriend issues, and the general coming of age that is associated with college life. We grow together, we make mistakes together, and in a lot of ways, we become men together.

We were used to leaning on each other in tough times and helping each other through hardships. This made me want to get back on campus and be with my team more than ever.

I sat in silent disbelief for what seemed like an hour.

Just months ago I was playing volleyball with Eddie. I was competing against him during 5:30 a.m. workouts. I was watching him run routes during spring practice. I was listening to him tell all of the defensive backs how none of us deserved to be on the field with him. He was one of the driving forces of our team, of our family. A linchpin. A motivator. A brother. Someone who made all of us better just by being present.

"Hey, McCann, you OK?" I heard from the doorway of the station.

"No," I said. "No, I'm not."

CHAPTER 06

TOGETHER, GRIEVING

WEDNESDAY, JUNE 22, 2005

ATLANTA, GA

CJ and I booked a flight to Atlanta from Jacksonville as soon as a date was set for the funeral. Though we thought a road trip in CJ's silver Lexus IS would be acceptable, our moms insisted on paying for flights. Nick Ellis arranged to pick us up from the airport and get us situated once we arrived. He and his parents welcomed the team into their home. Their generosity was an extension of Nick himself.

I can't say all of my teammates were men, most of us were boys and we acted like it. But Nick had something most of us didn't. He was a strong, humble man that would do anything for his brothers on the team. I had respect for Nick and how he approached his job on the field. He knew there were boundaries for kickers, but he knew how to earn respect. As he welcomed us out of the terminal, I couldn't help but look up to him.

"Hey guys, how was the flight in?" Nick's smile wasn't as broad as usual, nobody could blame him.

"Hey, buddy," I said, "bring it in." His hug was tight. The pat on the back that followed expressed his pain and appreciation for the team that was beginning to fill his home. His home became the unofficial meeting grounds for all of our teammates who could make it. CJ and I brought the total to double digits.

"Come here, CJ, you get one too."

"Hey, Nick, good to see you, man"

Being in Atlanta was surreal. None of us knew what to do. We all just stood awkwardly for a moment and stared at the ground as the weight of what we were about to face sank in. Eventually, we exchanged pleasantries with Nick's dad and packed our luggage into the back of the SUV.

"We should get going, got a bit of a drive," Nick was used to the uneasiness by now.

I drifted in and out of conversation as we drove through the outskirts of Atlanta and the windy roads of McDonough. Conversation was light; we still didn't have much to talk about.

Certain times in life silence is more comfortable than conversation. Sometimes you don't have the words. Other times you don't have the need. Today, we had neither. Being around other people who shared our emotion was comforting.

I thought about Nick and what he must have felt through all this. He and Eddie were such close friends. I knew Nick better than a lot of guys on the team and I knew he was hurting more than he'd show. He took special interest in me because I played soccer in high school and we shared something other than football. I never demeaned his position and I'd always congratulate him on extra points or field goals.

Nick Ellis was a leader, he just happened to play the position of kicker. Kickers don't always get the respect they deserve and Nick knew those stereotypes all too well. He'd been a kicker for years. He knew most football players picked on kickers and didn't consider them "part of the team" to some extent or another. This didn't bother Nick. He knew he had a job to do, and if he took care of his job, nobody could say anything to him. He didn't assert himself in the offensive or defensive huddles, but when special teams units needed to shine, he was ready and willing to be a vocal leader. He was one of the first people I saw who took responsibility for his actions. I couldn't help but admire his maturity.

As we drove through Atlanta, I could see Nick beginning to emerge as a leader. Not just a special teams leader, but a team leader. He had always been a leader in his own way, but today was different. Although the whole team wasn't here, he was strong when we were hurting. He welcomed us when we needed to come together. As I was unpacking my suitcase from the car, all I could think was Eddie would be proud of his friend right now.

When Nick decided to come to CSU, Eddie came with him. Coach Mills met Eddie while offering Nick a scholarship that fateful day in 2003, but didn't have room to offer him a scholarship. Eddie was talented, but not quite big enough. He had great hands, but he didn't have the speed. At the end of the day, Mills extended a preferred walk-on position to Eddie. No money, just a chance to earn a scholarship. That's all he ever needed. Eddie Gadson was on scholarship after the third game of his freshman season. Nick and Eddie had a special bond. Not many people come onto a collegiate sports program with a high school teammate. As freshmen they roomed together and as teammates they pushed each other. Eddie held for Nick during field goals and extra point attempts.

"He hated it. Oh man, he hated holding," Nick said as he cracked the first real smile all day. "He would always be tired after a drive and sometimes he just caught a touchdown pass, and now he had to hold for me. He'd be so upset."

The rest of us began joining in on the smiles. We couldn't help it, Nick was enjoying this story and it made us think about Eddie. Not in the same sad sense, but how we remembered him best.

"He'd come jogging back to me, taking his gloves off and mumbling under his breath, 'You better not miss this!' and I couldn't help but laugh at him. He was so serious, so competitive, but it loosened me up."

The joy in Nick's memory brought laughter to the rest of us. We were so torn about what to feel. All we'd done is mourn for the past week but all we had were fond memories of Eddie. The melancholy couldn't last forever. Nick's story finally broke through to us. We weren't miraculously healed of our grief, but we pulled together in those quiet moments at the Ellis home in McDonough, Georgia. We didn't need to say much about it, but we were all relieved to be back in the same room.

Like kids telling campfire stories, we sat and listened attentively, hanging on to his every word thinking about our friend. We were scattered about the living room strewn about on couches and chairs and carpet. Nick didn't want the attention on him, he wanted us to heal. But he knew he could help us do that in so many ways.

"He was so competitive, even at stuff he didn't love," tears couldn't stop the smile or the enthusiasm he had in the moment. "I'd take him out to play soccer-tennis, which is kinda like tennis but with a soccer ball and no racquet, and he'd beat me!" We all laughed and shook our heads, none of us were surprised to hear this gem. "Guys, I could have played soccer in college and after one game, he picks it up and figures out how to beat me." Nick shook his head and sat back in the wooden dining room chair that had been brought to the living room. "And it's not like I let him win either, he beat me fair and square, I was so upset."

I learned what real leadership under stress looked like that day. Many of us wanted to break down, some more than others. But we held each other up. Just as we had motivated each other through conditioning in the gym months before or just as we would push each other during workouts, we leaned on one another to get through the loss of a friend. Nick, though among the closest to Eddie, was the strongest. He bucked up and did everything in his power to serve his teammates when we arrived. He made us feel comfortable and ensured all of us got to the funeral.

He was hit harder than all of us, but he showed strength for us while we were there. Anybody can lead when things are smooth, but real leaders emerge when adversity strikes.

Later that day was the first time many of us had experienced death so close. Some of us had family or grandparents who had passed away, but few of us knew of someone our age that had been taken so suddenly. To say we were emotional would be an understatement. None of us said a word as the funeral began. That quickly changed when the preacher asked if anyone would like to share something about Eddie's life.

One by one, teammates walked up to the podium in the center of the room to talk about our friend. The family was not surprised when some of his best friends got up to talk. Guys who were close enough to shout "Hey!" to Eddie's parents when he was on the phone with them. Guys like Darius Jackson and Nick Ellis whose names the Gadsons had heard and who had deep friendships with their son. But each of us had been genuinely touched by this larger-than-life character and a number felt compelled to share.

Some shared how he had affected our lives in the locker room, in the weight room, or on the field. He was a remarkable person and if the people in the room didn't already believe that, we were out to convince them with story after story. Some talked about how one-on-one conversations motivated us, not just on the football field. As Darius put it, "Man to man, his conversations were impactful."

I talked about how he'd always deflect compliments after practice in the locker room. Nick spoke about how he was such an individual and how much he missed him. Just the other day they had been joking about who was going to make it to "The League" and buy a house on the beach. He shared how Eddie didn't always follow the rules. They played pickup basketball during football season and snuck to the military bases to play racquetball without the coaches' consent. I couldn't help but feel inspired by the stories that were being shared. Eddie was an incredible character and he'd left his mark on this world.

Edward A. Gadson
"Eddie"
October 7, 1984 – June 17, 2005

As I listened to the stories about this person who was destined for greatness, I thought about his life. I wished I knew him better. I wished I'd spent more time around him. He inspired me in the relatively small amount of time I'd known him. I could only hope that I could have this sort of impact on my team that he had on me.

Slowly, Mikey McCoy approached the pulpit to share his favorite memory. Mikey typically wore a mischievous grin, like he was planning a practical joke he wouldn't let you know about until he had pulled it off. But as he approached the stage his massive shoulders drooped and his smile was more than dull. I wasn't used to seeing Mikey in such nice clothes. His shirt was tucked in and his black tie was pulled loose enough for his large neck to breathe.

Most friends and family know you. But your teammates know you on a different level. How you push yourself and what sort of pain you're willing to endure says a lot about you. Mikey set out to explain, in a single story, the fire with which Eddie lived. A fire his parents knew well. He'd been driven since the time he could pick up a ball in between halves at his dad's Air Force base basketball games.

"In the spring of 2004," Mikey started, "we were coming off a terrible losing season. We only won one game. We were working out in the weight room and I wasn't taking it too serious." He pushed his hair out of his eyes every few words as he struggled to make eye contact with anyone. "I was joking around and having a good time, as usual. And then, this five-foot-nine, hundred and seventy pound receiver jumps in my face and starts chewing me out!" The glow of Mikey's smile was back.

A low rumble of belly laughs crept out from the crowd, particularly the football section on the right. Typical Eddie.

"I was twice this guy's size and a head taller than him, and he didn't care at all. He wasn't shy about what he had to say. He ripped me a new one and told me to get to work because he didn't want to have another losing season like that again. He was so competitive and he pushed us so hard. I've never had a teammate like Eddie. He made us all better when he was around." Mikey took one last sweeping glance through the room, "And that's the Eddie I remember."

I wondered how proud his parents must have been that their son, although only 20 years old, had become a man of such character. Someone that his teammates, his age and older, looked up to in so many ways. He was a competitor and a leader and although none of us could fathom the level of grief they were experiencing, we knew how important it was to share our Eddie stories.

Many of our teammates and coaches couldn't attend the funeral, but those of us who were fortunate enough to come poured out our hearts. During the funeral the Gadsons didn't say much.

But Paula, Eddie's Mom, left us with something at the wake we could never forget. The room froze when she stood. We hadn't heard from her or Eddie's dad all day. Her nose and cheeks were red from the tears she had been shedding for days. I couldn't begin to comprehend the sadness behind her tinted glasses. Through tears, emotional pauses, and her worn out handkerchief, she asked us one favor.

"We all had interactions with Eddie. Our son. And I want you all to do one thing." She paused to look at all of us. She seemed to make eye contact with everyone in the room. "If you ever heard Eddie say something he wanted to accomplish, pick up that one thing and do it. Do it so he can continue living vicariously through each of you."

Pride swelled through the football section. Heads nodded and jaws clenched – partially to hold back more tears and partially out of resolve. We decided then and there to honor our friend in whatever way we could. What if we could win something for Eddie?

CHAPTER 07

A PACT OVER KARAOKE

WEDNESDAY, JUNE 22, 2005

ATLANTA, GA

CJ Hirschman and I were best friends. The coaching staff knew it before we ever met. They knew we'd make great roommates and paired us up before we even stepped on campus. We both grew up in Jacksonville, we both came from football families, we both played in the secondary, and we were both business majors. Because we spent so much time together, girls even bought the lie that we were brothers.

I never saw it, but everyone else said we looked alike. I have hazel eyes, light brown hair and stood just over six feet. He was just a tad shorter with dark brown hair and painfully blue eyes that would charm girls into a coma with a single glance. His smile, sly and playful, didn't hurt him either. If he flashed it at you, you were under his spell. Guy, girl, old, young, it didn't matter. I witnessed CJ talk us into clubs and out of trouble more times that I could count. That evening, I had front row tickets for the show.

"Sorry guys, the kitchen is closed for the night," said the

waitress as she smacked her gum and dropped our water glasses on top of our drink coasters.

"Oh man, that sucks." I hadn't lifted my head from the menu before CJ had a lock on her. "What about appetizers? We're just in town for the night on business and we're starving. It's been a super-long day. Is there any way we can throw a couple things in? Nothing else around here serves food and this place looks awesome."

She had almost drooled on the table at this point. We were still in our clothes from the funeral so the "business trip" story was believable. She was just young enough and we looked just old enough for her to buy it.

"Ohhhh, okay, let me see what I can talk the kitchen into." Her smile was wide and her eyes were locked on him.

"So how did you get that super power again?" I rhetorically asked CJ as the waitress walked back to the kitchen.

He chuckled and took the wrapper off of his straw. "Cheers, sir," he said as he raised his glass, "to Eddie Gadson."

"To Eddie," I agreed.

This had been one of the most emotional 24 hours of either of our lives. We went from somber about Eddie's passing to excited about seeing our teammates to the mourning at the funeral. We were emotionally worn out and we had an early morning flight to catch. Nick and his parents offered to take us the next day, but we declined. They had done enough for us and they needed rest more than we did.

We sat in silence for a few moments before we realized everything that was going on around us. The restaurant, which was slowly transforming from a restaurant into a bar, was half full of young professionals and inebriated college-age kids. We fit right in.

One particularly comical guy was right behind us in the adjoining booth. CJ and I were already amused at how drunk this guy was from overhearing the conversation. Then the show began.

"Sunday Bloody Sunday" by U2 came over the speakers and we heard, "Oh this is my jam!" He was halfway sarcastic and halfway sounded like a drunken sailor. The table transformed into a drum set and his beer converted to a microphone. He proceeded to belt out every syllable, moan, and audible breath in the song. Bono himself could not have sung a better rendition!

We were impressed. CJ was a huge U2 fan, so we gave the guy a standing ovation, to which he humbly cheered his beer to us and chugged in his own honor. Drunk Karaoke Guy brought a smile to our faces and we welcomed the distraction on the emotional day.

"It's crazy to think how life just goes on after this," I said after our food had arrived.

"I know, crazy to think that it could have been any of us," CJ said with a mouthful of nachos.

"I wonder if Coach Mills will let us do the helmet stickers for Eddie," I said. "We should do something to honor him on our jerseys or something."

"I don't know, he won't let us have wrist bands or spat our cleats. I don't think he'll do anything to change our uniforms, but maybe t-shirts or something." He was the fastest eater on the planet. I'm not sure he chewed many of the nachos.

"Yeah, I don't know, I just hope he does it right. The biggest thing we can do is dedicate the season to him. If we won a conference championship in his honor? Nothing could top that. Eddie was so competitive, more than anything he would have wanted us to beat everyone in the conference."

This was the first time we'd talked about it out loud. A conference championship was a long way away and bold of us to believe, especially since we were 5-5 last year with only one conference win.

"It's gonna take a lot of work," I continued, "but we're gonna be so much better than last year."

"I know, a championship would be sick," his grin was wide as he imagined what that was like. "It's crazy to think how things work out. You thought you were going to Georgia Tech, I thought I was going to Stanford, Eddie was a walk-on, all the linebackers had other offers. And here we are. A bunch of misfits. We have the talent to do it; all of us had the chance to play at bigger schools. We just have to figure out how to put it all together."

I couldn't help but think of something Mom told me growing up, "Everything happens for a reason." The thought disappeared as quick as it came.

CJ and I made a pact that night to work as hard as we could to push our team to a conference championship. We could think of no better way to honor our friend than to dedicate a ring to him with the first winning season in school history.

CHAPTER 08

INTRO TO CAMP

SUNDAY, AUGUST 7, 2005

NORTH CHARLESTON, SC

"Quiet up!" I snapped before our meeting, the first of the year, was ready to start. Better me yell it than Coach Mills have to ask us to quiet down.

Coach Mills took the faux wood podium in the front left corner of the room with an impatient silence. He shuffled his loose leaf papers while the last of the team settled into their seats and locked eyes on him. Like a stick of dynamite with a burning fuse, he grew more discontent with every passing millisecond.

This was the dream he had wished for since he ditched his bright accounting career for coaching straight out of college. But, like many dreams that materialize, this wasn't how he pictured it. His dreams didn't include standing in front of his team with merely the tan line of a wedding band on his finger. His dreams didn't include giving the eulogy at the funeral for one of his favorite players. The lessons he'd learned this offseason and the ones he was still beginning to comprehend were invaluable. He was content with 2004, as many of his players were. But he, like them, wasn't satisfied.

If the small talk didn't dry up quick, he was not above taking the team out on the front lawn for up-downs in street clothes. This was his camp and he demanded respect. He knew what it would take to win games and he was ready to send a message.

The room settled and he opened the meeting with a welcome message sprinkled with scripture that set his expectations for the year. He referred to us as "champions" more than once, though we had yet to earn any such title. He attempted to put a positive spin on our mediocre season from the year before by calling us underdogs and explaining his strategy for "sneaking up on people" this year. He introduced the coaching staff and the administrators, each of whom bore mandatory messages from their respective departments about personal conduct, academics, and the Safe Harbor drug-testing program.

The Derry Patterson Wingo School of Nursing's sea foam green walls surrounded us on all four sides. Only 100 or so auditorium style seats occupied the room, just enough to fit the entire team plus some administrators under one roof. At the back of the room, the assistant coaches lined the pale green walls near the folding tables where we had just checked in. In the corner of the room stood administrators like Hank Small, the salt-and-pepper Athletic Director who, with a number of others, had helped Mills acquire the resources he needed for this season. And Christie Faircloth Dixon, the team's Student Athlete Success Coordinator who not only did her best to keep us academically eligible, but loved us as if we were her own bunch of rowdy teenagers.

The rows of collapsible chairs were filled with incrementally older players, the youngest starting back with the coaches and finishing with the seniors sitting directly in front of Mills. A large dry erase board covered the front wall of the room, something Mills was sure to utilize as he worked through the stack of papers he had in front of him.

Starting with Adam Degraffenreid, the Preseason All-Conference defensive end who sat in front of Mills, the seniors began introducing themselves to the room. Adam stood tall with his genuinely wide smile and addressed the team behind him, talking as much with his hands as his mouth, "Adam Degraffenreid, senior defensive end from Missouri by way of Butler County Junior College."

An awkward silence filled the classroom when the seat Tavares Shorter, who was printed on the cover of the media guide and my counterpart at the starting Spur position, should have occupied was passed over. Mills shook his head and made an aggressive mark in his notes while waving on the introduction ceremony.

A different kind of hush radiated when we came to the other open seat. This one belonged to Eddie. He would have been itching to get out of this air conditioned room and onto the field to catch balls, hurrying through this process as fast as he could. Coach Mills explained the intentionally empty seat with an emotional digression about how sorely we'd miss Eddie and how opportunity abounded for players to step up in his absence. Many of the freshmen were hearing the news of Eddie's death for the first time. He moved on with a business-like tone he over-emphasized, as if to try and fool us as well as himself that he was okay.

When the final cracking voices of freshmen attempting to sound tough were silenced, Coach Mills took on a more serious tone. The empty seat in which Eddie should have been sitting was not something to be passed over without elaboration. He talked about Eddie and how we would miss him, both on the field and off. The announcement segued into the release of our team's theme for the year. A mantra that would be a constant reminder that we don't just play for the people in the room with us now, but also for the one who was no longer with us. A saying we would wear on our shirts and we would repeat to each other all year, in jest and also with seriousness.

"Every Man, Every Play, Every Day" was not just something written on the whiteboard in front of us. The theme was something with which we identified. Before we left the meeting, each of us would sign the banner as a physical manifestation of our commitment to the team. We gave every bit of our physical ability to the team. We would push our bodies beyond their limits and encourage others to do the same. Our minds were no different, the only thing that consumed our thoughts were ways to get better and the schedule. The coaches made separate, but equal, secessions of their personal life and income.

Today, Coach Mills defined the purpose of our sacrifices. We would dedicate our season to Eddie and his family. Sitting in the collapsible auditorium chairs of the nursing building, we committed ourselves to accomplishing something larger than any of us individually could have taken on. Humility was required to admit no single person could do it on their own. Something most people outside of our cocooned world had trouble wrapping their minds around. We bought into the dream that we could be something more than just a football team who wins a few games. Everyone wants to do something huge with their life, this was our chance. The journey would not always be fun and sometimes the grind would be downright miserable, but we were all in it, together.

CHAPTER 09

LOCKER ROOM STENCH

MONDAY, AUGUST 8, 2005

NORTH CHARLESTON, SC

We could smell the musk from down the hall. Full on "stink" had yet to settle, but the smell was unmistakable. Years of blood, a few tears, and gallons of sweat had soaked into the carpets of the locker room. The scent grew more pungent as we neared the back of the athletic complex.

"Whew that is raw!" said CJ with a puckered face and a shake of his head.

"I know, right? I can smell it from here. Smells like…" I gave a dramatic pause for effect and lifted my nose to the air, "…dude."

I got a chuckle out of him as I thumbed the key code for entry. "Sometimes I think the coaches avoid shampooing the carpets on purpose. Like the smell is a 20-year history of the program." We both knew it wasn't true. The coaches did what they could with what they were given. Though they were not directly responsible for shampooing the carpet, they were given few resources and we often found Coach Kelly vacuuming the floors after practice. While

we sacrificed our bodies, they sacrificed their lives and their families'
lives to follow the dream of being a coach. During their first preseason camp, assistant coaches Perkins and Jamey Chadwell lived
in their cars for two weeks because they were too busy to secure
apartments. Coach Mills slept an average of 10 hours each week
during the season. Coming back on campus past midnight to see
a coach's car and fluorescent lights beaming through the stadium
offices was typical. They worked incredibly hard for meager salaries,
focusing more on winning and on the experience they gained than
the money they made. With the exception of Coach Kelly, who
"only wants to coach the O-line," each coach held aspirations to
someday become a head coach. We knew they weren't getting rich
and we appreciated their sacrifice.

"Ya never get used to this smell. I've been here all summer
and it still gets me." I was jealous CJ had stayed to work out this
summer and I hadn't. He had already told me how hard everyone was
working. I was lifeguarding on the beach in Florida while my
teammates lived and worked together. I scolded myself for staying
home and followed him into the den of dude.

The locker room was our safe haven. If we weren't in class,
we were likely here. Coaches mostly avoided the locker room and
we came here to get away from the distractions of student life.
The stories passed around in the locker room were usually filled
with jokes; some were true but most were exaggerated for the
crowd. Someone was constantly being picked on and some sort of
debate always seemed to be teetering on a fistfight. Arguments about
who was faster, which home state had better high school football
programs, or who could pull more girls were common.

What you couldn't hear were the one-on-one conversations. The guys who came to know Jesus in the locker room. The
guys who told the person next to them they just tore a ligament
and they'll be out the rest of the season. The guys who mentored
younger players about personal issues and expected playing time.

These close conversations are where I got to know Eddie

Gadson the previous year.

He and I had lockers near each other during my first year. As warring factions, defensive backs and receivers, our two position groups would beat each other up during practice. Then we would come back and decompress a foot apart from each other.

I learned about his character in those solitary conversations. I learned about his humble attitude and the way he was always striving to improve his game. He was one of the fiercest competitors I had ever known. He inspired me to get better and I was lucky to have a locker next to his for a year.

Eddie would not be next to me this season. The coaches made the decision to prepare Eddie's locker as it would look on game day with his game jersey, game pants, game socks, and game cleats all cleaned and laid out for him. They covered the locker with plexiglass, similar to a tomb filled with ancient artifacts, so it could not be disturbed. The plan was to keep it like that until he would have graduated. As I walked to my locker for the first time since school let out I stopped on locker number 21, Eddie's.

Now every time we walked by we would be reminded of Eddie. We knew some days it would be tough, especially for the guys that were closest to him. We also knew seeing that shrine would inspire us to never walk off that field unless we had given it our all, just as he would have done.

As I walked by, I remembered the talks we would have after practice. We were never that close, but in certain moments after extreme physical exertion, you can't help but bare your soul to whoever is around.

I'd call him "superstar" because of his performance on the field and the media attention he drew. As cocky as he was on the field, he was humble in those moments when someone would try to flatter him up close. He would deflect my compliments and turn it back on me, reminding me of something I did well at practice.

It's those little conversations that we would miss most about him. The way he made us feel. The way he would lift us up. The way he had the power to push us. Our turn to carry the baton had come. To continue his legacy and come together to accomplish something that nobody outside of our locker room could fathom.

I was back home with my team and camp was ready to begin. The carpet still stunk. But in that moment, as I sat in my locker reflecting on the events of the year, the smell was the most comforting thing I could imagine. I couldn't think of any place I'd rather be.

CHAPTER 10

HOLDING

TUESDAY, AUGUST 9, 2005

NORTH CHARLESTON, SC

Ask any football player about preseason camp and we'll give you something chocked full of mixed emotions. It was miserable, yet it was a challenge we longed for. It was difficult, but it was fun. The schedule was unrelenting, but we narrowed our focus. We pushed ourselves to exhaustion and it tested our will. You found out what you were made of during fall camp. You were nervous, anxious, and excited all at once.

From the first day we put on pads, we were physically and mentally challenged. Those challenges didn't stop until a week prior to the first game of the season. Most mornings we woke up so sore it hurt to get out of bed. Everything from our necks to our toes and everything in between ached on a daily basis.

Our heads hurt from dehydration and lack of rest. Our necks hurt from slamming into each other like mountain goats for hours every day. Our shoulders and backs hurt from holding up shoulder pads and throwing our bodies into other grown men at top speeds.

Our fingers were gashed from endlessly fighting off opponents and our bodies were covered in random scrapes from being bashed into the ground. To put it lightly, showers stung.

And our legs. Our legs were exhausted from nonstop running. We jogged during warm-ups, we sprinted in drills, we hustled to drills, we backpedaled in drills, we shuffled, and then... then we conditioned. Conditioning consisted of either 110-yard sprints or gassers across the field. Conditioning came at the end of practice when we were mentally, physically, and emotionally spent. It was a test of manhood, an evaluation to see how far we would go on empty tanks. To see who would give up and who would push through the pain.

A thin line lies between being injured and being hurt. You're injured? Go see an athletic trainer and get back out here as soon as possible. You're hurt? Great, we all are; quit whining and keep going. Pushing through that pain is a lesson I'll never forget. Clichéd mottos from the coaches like "If it were easy everyone would do it" were unimaginably accurate. Without the pain of the offseason and preseason workouts, nothing could prepare us for the pain necessary to push through exhaustion during a game.

Most people don't go through such physically demanding trials. We were fortunate to do so. It taught us to be mentally strong. It taught us that no matter how much it hurts, the choice to ignore the pain sat in our own heads. Enduring hardship is a choice. And learning to endure is a skill we relentlessly sharpened during camp. Conditioning taught us to push through pain. Lots of people go through life and attempt to take the easy way out. In preseason camp, an easy way out is a fairy tale. Everyone is stressed and everyone hurts, but we band together to get the job done.

During preseason camp I learned to push the guys around me. I never let them get away with "just enough" because I knew others would keep me just as accountable. I learned to stop focusing on how much my body ached and aim whatever leftover energy I still had toward my teammates. Encouraging them. Lifting them up.

Joking with them. Praising them. When I stopped thinking about my own pain and focused on lifting others up, the pain disappeared.

Although conditioning wasn't scheduled till after practice, I had someone to lift up right now.

"You ready to get started?" I said to Nick. He was anxious. Or nervous. Or sad. I could see it from across the practice field through the morning mist. Maybe he was thinking about kicking with a new holder. Maybe he was thinking about the fresh ink of the tattoo on his back commemorating our friend. Maybe he was thinking that the balls were going to be wet because of the dew on the field. Maybe he was just focused.

The morning dew laid on the grass like a thin layer of icing, ready to be kicked away with every footstep. Droppings left by the Canada Geese that lived on campus were nestled in the grass like little sprinkles on a cake. Circles and lines and zig-zags of footprints covered the field where overly ambitious players like Nick and me were already warming up. Because of our lack of lights on the practice field and our need to avoid the unrelenting heat of midday, our first two-a-day practice started in 15 minutes at 7:00 a.m. sharp.

"Ready as I'm gonna be," he said with a forced smile behind his facemask. He jogged toward me drawing a new path in the wet grass, fully suited and ready to start kicking. Nick stood five foot eight, but like everyone, seemed taller in pads.

I braced myself for the conversation. Eddie Gadson not being with us for the first days of camp brought on a melancholy attitude to the team. He would normally be running his mouth to the defensive backs or having fun with some of the offensive guys. The hot, humid air felt different. We were missing something. Missing someone.

Eddie held a huge place in the offense and there were a number of guys that needed to step up to fill the void. But he played on many special teams as well. Along with returning punts, he was the placeholder for Nick on field goals and extra points.

Eddie and Nick went to high school together and Eddie had been Nick's holder for years. I was the place holder for our high school kicker so Nick trusted I had the skills for the position. On top of that, I'd always treated Nick with respect, something that not all kickers earned as quickly as other players. Trusting a place holder is extremely important for a kicker. The kicker has to put faith in the holder to get the ball snapped, catch it, place it on the ground at the right angle, and move his hands in less than two seconds. If I didn't get that job done, Nick would whiff and pull a muscle or he'd kick me, inevitably breaking something in his foot or my hand. Nick and I developed a quick bond from the pressure we put on ourselves. I took the job with pride, knowing I had a chance to step up in Eddie's absence in a small way.

I couldn't replace the Sundays Nick spent with Eddie holding kicks and catching punts. Partly because I couldn't catch a punt to save my scholarship. But mostly because that faith in each other is hard to build. Nick and Eddie would kick for hours outside of our team practices. They'd practiced back home and they'd practiced in the offseason. Nick was coming off his best statistical year with Eddie at his foot and I had a lot of ground to make up. Not only did I have to learn the technicalities of how Nick wanted me to hold, but I had to earn his trust.

His eyes finally met mine as he gave me five and patted me on the shoulder. He took off his helmet to reveal his shaved head and dark brown eyes.

"I know this might be a little weird for you, but I'm coachable so tell me exactly how you want me to hold," I said.

"I will, buddy," he began as he collected footballs. "Eddie was my best friend, but I'll tell you what, he really didn't like holding. He always called it a 'chore,' especially after he scored a touchdown!" We shared a laugh as we piled up the balls near the extra point indicator on the field. "He would say, 'I'm sick of doing this, I can't stand it,' and then he'd plop down and we'd score some points."

"Left leg back?" I asked as he placed his right toe at my fingertips on the soggy grass.

"Yep, just like that, lean back in a bit. There ya go. You know I'm thinking it, but I'll do my best not to say, 'That's not how Eddie did it,' to ya."

I gave him a smile, "Well... I'll do my best not to make you want to say something like that!" He nodded his head, signaling he was ready. "Get set, get set, get set."

I checked back with Nick before I gave him the first fake snap of the morning. He was focused. His eyes didn't meet mine, they were locked on the fingers of my left hand, planted in the ground. He was ready to strike, ready to get the nervousness out.

"Blue!" I said in a gruff tone, acting out the exact motions I would use in a game situation. I mocked an incoming snap and lowered the ball to the ground where my left hand was placed.

THUD

Nick's foot struck the ball clean, "Nice job, Nick. Do it again."

CHAPTER 11

A SPECIAL GUEST

FRIDAY, AUGUST 12, 2005

NORTH CHARLESTON, SC

Ed Gadson stood between the asphalt parking lot and the trimmed edge of the practice field. This was the first time we'd seen each other since the funeral. Though his athletic frame stood tall, his shoulders drooped just the slightest bit. He couldn't decide whether to hold them behind his back like he'd been trained in the Air Force or stuff them into the pockets of his cargo shorts. We watched from an entire field away, but his body language said it all. This was one of the toughest things he's ever done in his life. Something he didn't have to do.

He came to town to visit the team and stayed with his loyal friend Mitch, who attended numerous home games. Mitch and his wife Peggy were like family. Mitch was the local friend who checked on Eddie his freshman year after a basketball injury left him with a broken bone in his face just days after his parents, still stationed in Japan, received the news over an Internet broadcast at 2:00 a.m. that Coach Mills was planning to put him on a full scholarship. He was the friend who helped convince Ed to restrain Paula from purchasing a plane ticket from Japan, their son was in good hands. She didn't want her baby to be alone during a time of pain. No parent could blame her for wanting to make the trip. The next time she wanted to get to her baby in his time of suffering she was too late. Her conscious bore the burden of that realization every day.

Paula didn't come to practice and she wasn't sure if she'd come to any more games; being on the field brought back too many memories. Memories of being his coach in youth football, which ran the risk of embarrassing her son, and experiencing the joy typically reserved for fathers. She couldn't bear to rehash the times he looked out for other players like little Justin on that same youth football team, players who were not as gifted as him, but who he still wanted to see succeed. After all, they were his friends. Memories of Eddie, playing in both college and in little league, becoming infuriated when a coach took him out of the game. His competitive fire was sparked early.

Ed glanced as defensive linemen slammed into each other in tackling drills. The defensive backs angled back and forth connecting orange cones with precise, backwards sprints. He saw the herd of offensive linemen kicking up dust near the pond like an angry stampede of elephants. He heard Coach Kelly harp on the "Z in the knee" as they stomped back into their stances. The running backs practiced pass protection while linebackers came barreling down on them from staged blitzes. The entire team wore the same uniform of black cleats, white socks, gold pants, and a jersey indicating their respective side of the ball; white for offense, blue for defense. Not a single arm band or spatted cleat could be found. The only single piece of flair allowed by Mills was a black dot reading "EG21" on the back of each helmet. Ed watched the other half of the "Collin and Eddie Show" zip balls during Pass Skeleton. Passes that landed in the hands of players like Maurice Price and Ryan Robertson, guys he had heard stories about over the phone so many times.

But Eddie wasn't there to catch any passes.

Eddie and Ed had shared sports since Eddie could barely grip a ball with two hands, much less one. His greatest joy as a father came when his son carried out his dream to play Division 1 football. He missed Eddie's smile, his companionship, his laugh, he even missed the headaches. More than anything, he missed being Eddie's dad.

Ed was out of town visiting a friend when he received the call from Paula that changed his life. The last time he saw Eddie was when they played 18 holes of golf together, mere days before the accident. He remembered it plain as day, like a picture. They headed down the last fairway before the sunset. They chose to walk so they had to hurry because they wanted to play the last hole before sunset.

Ed Gadson appreciated the fact that we had chosen to dedicate the season to Eddie. He knew to memorialize his son in a way that only we could do, with a trophy earned playing the game his son loved so much, was the greatest gift we could provide as a team. He told us much of this in a brief address to the team following practice that afternoon. His strength gave us strength. No matter how hard the sun beat down, no matter how tired we thought we were, nothing compared to what he was enduring. Our physical burdens seemed a bit lighter after Ed came to visit.

CHAPTER 12

IDENTITY

SATURDAY, AUGUST 13, 2005

NORTH CHARLESTON, SC

I couldn't believe my eyes. Marvin was doing push-ups. He wasn't taking advantage of the 30 seconds rest we were given. Not only that, he was ridiculing everyone who looked tired!

Marvin McHellon was a guy everyone enjoyed being around; nobody had a reason to dislike him. In position meetings we'd tease that he was a 60-year-old man in a 20-year-old's body because he was so much wiser than the rest of us. He was humble and he was smart, always the consummate servant leader. He let his actions do most of the talking but was still willing to be verbal when needed. When he told us to hustle up or broke up fights, the guys he reprimanded had no reason to carry grudges. Like me, he was a defensive back. Out of all the guys on the team, I looked up to him the most.

Marvin stood 5'9" and weighed a lean 185 pounds when he arrived for camp. His dreadlocks were well kept and thin, falling below his shoulders if taken out of the mandatory beehive of a bun hanging at the nape of his neck. The school, disapproving of his hair, asked that it be kept in a bun when on campus or cut. His hair seemed to grow by the day, forcing him to wear a helmet that was normally reserved for 300 pound linemen. From the side, all I could see was the tattoo on his arm glossed in sweat and a mass of hair bobbing up and down like some sort of machine stuck on overdrive. Meanwhile, I forced myself to breathe in through my nose and out through my mouth in an attempt to keep up.

Practice was over, but conditioning was just beginning. Full contact 3-on-3 and Oklahoma drills had already worn us down. We had already shed our shoulder pads and most of us were only wearing helmets above the waist. Some of us even opted to toss our hip and butt pads, just for comfort's sake. Less clothing meant less weight. Less weight meant you move faster. Strict time requirements to get to the far side of the field and back were assigned. Our position group, "Skill" had only 18 seconds. If someone didn't make it, the rep didn't count. Gassers, ugh.

When Coach Mills arrived two years ago, he attempted to give the team the personality he wanted. He had always envisioned his team to be "old school." One that could be transported to the era of Bear Bryant or Vince Lombardi and stand the test of time. He wanted us to be tough and play tough, using a variety of quotes and stories from these legendary coaches in an attempt to motivate us. Unfortunately, 2003 didn't set that tone and 2004 proved that our team personality was one of finesse instead of power. When my class arrived en masse in 2004, we arrived to a team without much of an identity.

Guys like Marvin were thrown into the fire as leaders at young ages, even though they were still figuring things out for themselves. They knew who they didn't want to be. They didn't want to be the team that lost all but one game. Mills faced a different, but just as daunting, challenge in his second year due to the massive influx of new faces. We all came from separate backgrounds and the culture that had been established the previous year was weak at best. Every first-year coach faces this tough exercise of figuring out who their team should be. Coach Mills witnessed this process two years in a row due to so many new players.

During the 2004 season, he continually harped on us, professing that we were an "old-school football team." He'd make clichéd comparisons to the likes of the Steel Curtain and the Super Bowl-winning Packers of the Lombardi dynasty. He saw something in us we didn't see when we looked into the mirror. Like a mom who wants her child to be a beauty queen contestant because her time had passed, Mills wanted us to be something we didn't think we were cut out for.

Every football team wants to be known as hard-nosed, but if that's not the style of play that it utilizes, it won't become some self-fulfilling prophecy. Most "old-school football teams" employed run-heavy offenses with a big tight end and light passing game. In reality, we ran a high-passing percentage offense with a meager ground game. We played a 3-3-5 on defense, using three down linemen, three linebackers, and five defensive backs. This gave us more skill players on the field than large bodies. This scheme naturally implied we would beat teams with our speed rather than size and strength.

We were tough, but we weren't an old school football team. In a private meeting with Coach Mills I shared many of my teammates' concerns about his vision for us. He was understanding and took my words to heart more than I expected. He let me speak as a man and he valued my opinion, something that taught me to speak my mind when I felt strong about an idea. This year, he had yet to make worn out comparisons we didn't think fit us. We had a team identity, but this one belonged to us.

"11 - 12 - 13 - 14 - 15," Marvin was still going. Meanwhile, the rest of us could barely stand up. He was setting the pace, something we needed. The air was so full of humidity you had to chew it just to fill your lungs. Marvin remembered that one-win 2003 season and the comparisons of old. He wanted to create a new identity for this team. One that was infused with this work ethic and a competitive spirit. He wasn't about to settle for less, not this year.

As I watched him pouring sweat, I noticed teammates respond to his words and his actions. I contributed a few encouraging claps to add to the positivity. We were a different team than last year. Something in our attitudes had changed, something I couldn't fully gauge. Our identity was no longer a group of individuals playing together, we had become one team. Nobody was scowling at Marvin for making them look bad, something that may have happened in years prior. They took his words as encouragement and stood tall. We didn't fight the difficulty of the situation. We leaned into it with everything we had left. We were becoming unified. I learned how to lead from watching Marvin push us with his push-ups.

BEEEP

"Come on fellas, let's go!" Somehow he made it out of the push-up position and was out ahead of me. "We gotta work harder! Those Bulldogs and Keydets will be waiting for us!" he said, referencing The Citadel and Virginia Military Institute. "We gotta be in better shape this year!"

Camp was in full swing.

CHAPTER 13

FLASHBACK

SATURDAY, OCTOBER 2, 2004

NORTH CHARLESTON, SC

Marvin remembered, as many of my older teammates did, what losing all those games felt like. The losses gave them more of an appreciation for the wins we secured in 2004. Throughout camp he continually referenced the game we played against the Virginia Military Institute Keydets.

Coach Mills often talked about "turning over the flywheel," an analogy he used to encourage us when the future seemed bleak. A flywheel, as he explained, was like a circus ride or a toy you'd see on an executive's desk that has to build momentum by being pushed back and forth until finally it flips over and carries itself. The object, our team in his analogy, required work to get moving, but once it flipped over the momentum carried the object around and around with minimal effort. Before the game he talked about how close we were to getting the flywheel to turn over; aka how close we were to winning.

Old school football coaches, like my Dad, talk about "perfect football weather" in the fall. The temperature hovers around 70 and clouds are nearly impossible to find. A light breeze blows just enough to keep players cool, but not so much that it shifts the ball in the air. Coaches can wear long-sleeves but players can forgo the layers.

A year prior, when we stepped onto the field with the VMI Keydets, we didn't have perfect football weather; we had perfect beach weather.

The temperature was just a hair above 90 and the humidity was so thick you could taste it. We didn't even have a fully functioning scoreboard, much less lights so games started at 1:30. The sun beat down hard enough for fans to get a tan or pass out from heat exhaustion while they watched. Like mops, our white jerseys and gold pants gathered sweat even before warm-ups.

A full row of seats was hard to find in the stadium. Only 2,000 fans braved the stifling heat to cheer us on. No matter, the lackluster atmosphere was part of our counter-intuitive home field advantage. We lulled teams to sleep. We were used to not having many fans so playing without noise was a normal part of our Saturday routine.

The dense humidity added injury to insult as the Keydets went to work on us for the first three quarters of the game. They were prepared for everything we threw at them. Offensively we were minimally effective and defensively we could barely slow them down. As Coach Kelly would say with his deep Mississippi accent, "They were ready for a dawg fight."

VMI approached their trip south to Charleston as just another road trip. Rightfully so, we had done nothing to warrant any sort of intimidation. We, on the other hand, had circled the game on our calendars as our first opportunity to beat a conference opponent. The disciplined strategist, Mills made an audacious move most men would never consider.

He knew, because he studied the previous years' games, that VMI lost steam during their last trip to North Charleston in 2002.

He watched the film and noticed that they lost momentum in the second half of the game. A weather delay helped the Keydets rehydrate and eventually win the game. But he identified their weakness: they weren't conditioned for the heat and humidity of the deep South.

With one of his most strategic moves, Coach Mills exercised his option to tell the Keydets that we would wear white uniforms that day, not them. The home team typically wears dark colors, but technically we had the option to choose. We chose white. Meanwhile, they were forced to wear their red and yellow uniforms that attracted significantly more heat than ours.

But on that scorching day last season it didn't seem to matter. Dark uniforms or light, we still trailed 24-3 just minutes into the fourth quarter. We looked like a team who was ready to give in. We had been beaten up since the first whistle and our spirit was all but broken. Internally, we put so much emphasis on the game that this sort of loss would devastate us.

But we had reason to hope. We could see VMI waning across the sauna of a playing field. Their jerseys were drenched and they were beginning to walk to the line of scrimmage when they'd previously been sprinting. They got up slower every time we made a tackle, and their enthusiasm faded. They deserved to be tired, they had been pounding us for three quarters non-stop.

Out of nowhere, a small spark was ignited. Eddie Gadson returned a punt seven yards to put us on our own 30-yard line. We completed seven passes to Maurice Price, Dimar Labega, and Collin's favorite target that year, Eddie. We thought about asking ourselves where this sort of dominance came from, but we knew better. Instead of jinxing the momentum, we swam directly into it.

The wave of momentum swelled on our sideline as we kicked off to the Keydets. I kept hearing Coach Barrows say, "Men they're tired! Look at the body language, they don't want to go back out there with you! Let's go out there and get the ball back for the offense so they can do it again!" He had us ready to break through a brick wall.

A quick three and out later, we had the ball on our own 47. Mills, also the offensive coordinator and play caller, didn't waste any time. He saw the opportunity and we struck. Two passes to Eddie, two rushes, and an extra point later, we were within seven points of the Keydets. We shrunk their lead from three touchdowns down to one with back-to-back drives.

24-17, Keydets.

Barrows yelled, "Do it again! Do it again!" from the sidelines as the defense took the field. We were mentally and physically prepared for a brawl in that next drive. The feeling of exhaustion had been replaced by the competitive spirit we each possessed. Encouragement flowed from the sideline and we fed each other's energy up like never before. Adam Degraffenreid, a junior defensive end with big play potential, and the linebackers made quick work of the weakened Keydets. We forced a three and out and made VMI punt for the third time in a row.

When Eddie Gadson made a fair catch with his heels on our 40-yard line, there was exactly 2:10 left on the clock. 60 yards lay ahead of us. Mills offensive system is designed for quick passes and small gains. Perfect for the situation. We needed to get out of bounds to make the clock stop. If we couldn't complete a pass, we'd still have the clock stopped for us. Week after week after week, Mills made us practice "Two Minute Drill," promising us we would need it someday.

The situation wasn't new to us. Everything we'd practiced led us to that single drive. The conditioning, the relentless reps of special situations, and the attention to detail Coach Mills shoved down our throats. It all came down to this drive and we were more than prepared.

The drive started off with four completions chunking off 48 yards and ticking away all but a minute off the clock.

Coach Mills called two running plays in a row, counting on

the clock to burn down. What he didn't count on was the two false starts that put us back at the 14-yard line. Now, third and 12 with the first down marker inconveniently placed on the two-yard line, 30 seconds were left on the clock and we could feel the momentum building like a wave, ready to crash down onto the goal line at any moment.

We held hands and silently said prayers as we pressed together to get the best view from the sideline. In our excitement, we spilled out of the designated sideline box onto the field and the referees threatened us with a sideline infraction. Nervousness came over us and adrenaline pumped through every vein in our bodies. At any moment something could go terribly wrong and the game would be over. At the same time we were invincible. Time slowed down and nothing mattered except winning the game.

Collin had his choice of weapons and went with true freshman Maurice Price. Price, an incredible athlete and perfect complement to Eddie's possession-driven game, came down with the ball to bring us within one point, 24-23. All we had to do was kick an extra point and we'd send the game to overtime. They couldn't hang with us, they were too wiped out. We couldn't lose in overtime, it was our day!

Except, Coach Mills had other plans. He wasn't interested in overtime, he was interested in winning. With 28 seconds left on the clock, Coach Mills signaled the boldest call in CSU football's 20 year history, a two-point conversion. He wanted to make a statement to VMI and the Big South that day. He wanted to announce that these were not the CSU Buccaneers of 2003. This was a new team.

"Orbit" was a play we practiced every week, sometimes multiple times each week. A trick play that involved a pre-snap shift with the tight end in motion. If the defense wasn't ready, they would be misaligned and our tight end would be wide open.

On defense, we'd seen this a hundred times in practice. So from the sideline, we knew what was about to happen. We gripped each other's hands on the sideline and watched with the utmost focus.

Coach Mills couldn't help it, he approached everything strategically. On the headsets in between plays as the drive progressed, a different conversation was happening that none of us knew about. Coach Jamey Chadwell, an offensive assistant, wanted to put John Muller, a senior, in at tight end instead of Bryan Meers. Muller had better hands, no question. But Meers was one of the guys Mills recruited. He epitomized hard work, staying after practice each day for no less than 20 minutes to work on his ball-catching ability. Some days he'd catch passes from Collin or a backup quarterback. But on most days he stood feet from the JUGS machine, typically reserved for launching punts into the air, catching balls. A coach would shoot balls at him so fast he had to wear a helmet in case one slipped through his hands, otherwise he'd end up with a broken nose.

"Bryan Meers has no history of the knowledge of the program," said Mills. "He doesn't know he's supposed to drop this ball. Yes, John Muller has better hands, we know that. But it's time to pass the torch."

End of discussion. Bryan Meers was going to make the winning catch. In the past we could never figure out a way to complete games. We played well, but didn't finish. We possessed potential, but never performed. John Muller had been in the program years before I was here or before Coach Mills came onto the scene. Mills chose Meers, a junior college transfer who had joined the team less than one year prior to this experience. Coach Mills was doing his best to usher in a new era. He had nothing against John Muller. He was a dependable tight end and a great leader. But he wanted Bryan Meers to have the opportunity to win it for us.

As the ball left Collin's right hand it seemed to hang in the air for an eternity. Orbit worked perfectly. Meers was wide open and his hard work paid off. 25-24, Bucs.

VMI attempted a comeback, but like a car running on fumes,

they had nothing left to give. They employed a running offense and couldn't complete any passes with the remaining seconds. Our win against VMI was the first victory against a conference opponent, a turning point for the program.

When Coach Mills gave his postgame speech, we were all smiles. He had been talking to us all year about "turning the flywheel." Our hard work in the off-season, the conditioning in preseason, and the tough losses we'd already faced were all pushes we had to make before we could get the flywheel to turn over. He closed with a simple statement that caused the entire locker room to go nuts, "Men. Today, the flywheel turned over!"

Collin completed 29 of 42 passes for over 300 yards and two

Coach Mills, eager to improve the school's facilities (note the scoreboard with missing bulbs) and begin a winning tradition, was ecstatic to earn the program's first Big South Conference victory against VMI in 2004.

TD's. Eddie and Price each caught a touchdown and they combined for over 150 receiving yards. Two other receivers, Dimar Labega and a senior named Harry Seabrook, also had great days. Bryan Meers only caught one ball, the most important of the game.

On defense, another two seniors Bowe Butler and Devin Maffett each brought in 11 tackles. Adam Degraffenreid, who was beginning to get some attention as a playmaker, brought down five tackles and a crucial sack.

The most impressive stat of them all was seven. VMI had so many players go into full body cramps after the game, our athletic training staff was forced to use all seven of our IV's on them. I came into the Athletic Training Center after the game to get ice on my bruised body, only to find it packed with their red and yellow uniforms in the fetal position. I sat in awe of the wincing faces and the drenched jerseys that filled the room. Despite the Keydets emptying their tanks, we still won. We played a complete game and we wore VMI out. That victory last season was the day our program turned the corner.

The win against VMI came only because of great effort. Effort Marvin knew needed to be topped this year.

CHAPTER 14

THE CHARLESTON CHOKE

WEDNESDAY, AUGUST 17, 2005

NORTH CHARLESTON, SC

Every one of my West Coast teammates would feel it 10 times worse than us East coasters. They were used to the cool, dry air of Southern California. Where "the real USC is," or so they would constantly remind University of South Carolina fans. Endless arguments over which school, Southern California or South Carolina, should be called "USC" waged each week. During the Charleston summers, a solid wall of humidity wraps around your skin like a wetsuit covering every inch of your body as soon as you step outside. As a result, we were always sweating. In class, walking to The Caf, and especially at practice. It always came thickest during camp, when an escape to the air conditioning was impossible.

We called it "The Charleston Choke."

It would turn 87-degree days into 101-degree days before noon. The Choke caused us to be drenched in sweat before we made it to the practice field. The Choke is what made guys collapse into full body cramps. It sucked, but it also helped us beat teams like

VMI in the fourth quarter.

We were used to The Choke because we spent hours and hours in the thick of it leading up to the season. We spent every possible minute of practice we could in the scorching heat and muggy humidity. We needed the advantage come Saturday afternoon. We loathed the heat, but we knew necessary evils stood between us and winning.

Practice took tolls on our bodies, causing us to lose fluids as fast and as severe as a sponge being wrung dry. Athletic training protocol demanded that we weigh in before and after each practice to determine how much water weight we lost. Had preseason camp been a weight loss program, results would be astounding. Three or four pounds was normal but eight or nine on a blistering day wasn't a surprise to anyone.

Tiny sweat beads covered my back and my hair dripped with perspiration. Wearing only a soaked pair of practice pants and some tape on my wrists, I stepped my bare feet onto the cold scale.

"Let's see where you're at Mr. McCann," said Toby Harkins, the head athletic trainer, in a concentrated tone. He was well versed in the art of sarcasm, but didn't have time for nonsense right now, he had to weigh in 90 athletes. He read the digital scale aloud, "198.7."

My eyes widened, "Uh oh." I was about to get an earful.

"Mike, that's 13 pounds," his voice stern. "How did you lose this much? Were you not drinking during practice? You know you can't go tomorrow if you don't gain 90 percent of this back, right? You cannot be doing this to me..." his voice trailed off as he walked down the hall to enter my weight on the chart that spanned the length of the hallway. He murmured something about needing me to lead under his breath as he scribbled in my weight at the cross section of today's date and my name.

He was right, I didn't drink enough at practice. I hated to show "weakness" by slurping up water. I tried to be the last one to drink and the first one to every drill. I wanted to keep up with guys like Marvin.

"You know what this means right?" He was back in my face. His shaved head was in my line of sight and the blue eyes looking up at me were like steel. His face was red from the sun and his hands were on his hips, waiting for me to take him seriously. Camp takes a toll on all of us, even the ones who aren't in pads.

"It means I was fat and kind of out of shape when I got here?" I kept him waiting as I stepped off the scale and began unraveling the tape off of my wrists.

"Seriously, do you know what you have to do?" A look came over him that pleaded with me to tell him what he wanted to hear. Normally he would playfully banter with me. He wasn't in the mood for jokes.

"Yes, sir. Lots of fluids and plenty of food. I need to get back to 90 percent of 213…"

"That's 209.1," he interrupted with specificity, "or else you don't practice tomorrow. Got it?"

"Yes, sir," I said with a nod and a salute to exaggerate my understanding.

"Next!" he yelled in my face as he walked back to the scale. He shook his head and finally cracked a smile as I turned and walked back to the locker room.

Finally, I was starving.

As much as I joked with him, I knew Toby was right. I had to get re-hydrated. He was serious about me not practicing if I didn't gain back my weight. I showered and put on my standard yellow shirt and navy shorts before CJ and I jumped in my white Ford Escape. We picked up a handful of freshman without cars walking through the parking lot and sped across campus to The Caf. I felt bad for the guys who couldn't ride but we piled in as many as we could before we left. We limped in tired and hungry and ready to eat. The tasty stuff ran out quick so we had to get in early before the masses arrived.

With blue plastic trays full of water, Gatorade, and mounds of chicken, I headed to meet CJ, Jon Carmon, and David "Mish" Misher at their table.

Like CJ and me, David and Jon always seemed to hang out together. They went to the same high school, they both played cornerback, and they always seemed to be arguing about something. Their own debates were funny to watch, but God help you if they ganged up on you. I tried not to enter into too many heated discussions; I'd be crushed by their superior debate skills.

"You alright, Biff?" Jon asked as I sat down my tray, mockingly using my high school nickname he had picked up over the summer from CJ. "Cause you look terrible!" All three of us rewarded his joke with a chuckle as I plopped down in the chair.

"Yeah, I'm alright. I lost a ton of weight, though. I have to drink a bunch of fluids," I explained as I downed my first cup of water.

"Be careful," said David as he stuffed a chicken finger into his mouth, "don't want Toby to get that rectal thermistor out."

"I know, right," I said with caution as I unwrapped the melted bag of ice from my lower back, "that would suck if I caught a full body cramp right now."

It happened every year. We would lose one of our own to the humidity. A falling out was never season-ending, but you were scarred for life if you went down from the heat with a full-body cramp. A full-body cramp has been described to me as every muscle in your body tensing up as tight as it can possibly pull. Your abs cramp, then your pecs follow shortly after. Your legs curl up into your abdomen, your fists clench, and your arms cross on your chest. You end up in the fetal position, whether you like it or not. You cannot move and everything painfully cramps as your body screams for hydration.

Just as we were joking about cramps, we heard a loud crash.

We turned to see who dropped their tray and found a freshman linebacker laying on the ground slowly curling up into the fetal position as if in an ironic response to our conversation.

"Man down! Man down!" Jon Carmon jumped out of his chair and ran over to the linebacker whose name I hadn't yet learned. "Oh man, you alright? You crampin up?" Jon said, his earlier jokester persona replaced by obvious concern we weren't used to seeing in him.

Food was scattered everywhere and four cups of liquid slowly spread across the stone floor. The linebacker's body shrunk into itself as his muscles tightened. If pain was weakness leaving the body, pretty soon he was going to be the strongest dude on the team.

Marvin, Jon and some of the older guys in the area started helping the Freshman to his feet. They immediately escorted him back to the Athletic Training Center, ATC for short, where Toby and his team would dump him into the cold tub and check his core temperature. We all said a little prayer for our teammate. The other freshmen watched with wide eyes, afraid to move a muscle out of fear of cramping themselves. They had never seen anything like this and didn't know what was happening.

Someone behind me whispered, "What are they gonna do with 'em?"

I turned around to see Eli Byrd, my high school teammate, with eyes and mouth wide open. "They'll take him to the ATC, dump him in the cold pool, pump him full of Bana – that hydration stuff – and water until he's feeling better. Then they'll have to gauge his core temperature with a rectal thermistor before he can practice again."

Eli's eyes widened to a cartoonish size.

"That's a thermometer in his butt," David clarified bluntly as all of us had a chuckle. All of us except Eli, of course. "Get yo weight up so you don't end up like him Byrd Man," David said as he toasted his Gatorade filled plastic cup in Eli's direction.

"I'll be right back," I said as I got up from the table. "I need some more water."

CHAPTER 15

A TIME TO MOURN

SATURDAY, AUGUST 20, 2005

NORTH CHARLESTON, SC

The stagnant air of Lightsey Chapel, the campus auditorium, brimmed with sadness. We entered through the back foyer and made our way down the maroon aisles toward the center seating in the lower deck. The stage was sparsely set with a sleek, black grand piano and a few risers for the non-existent chorus. The gothic organ pipes, set in the faux balcony boxes on either side of the empty room, gave the room more of a church feel than that of an auditorium.

None of us were in a hurry for the message we were about to hear. Reggie and I picked our folding seats next to each other and simultaneously exhaled a forceful breath as we settled in. I rubbed my legs through my shorts, partly out of soreness and partly out of anxiousness. It's not that we didn't want to be there; it's that we knew this was going to be tough.

Most of the team and coaching staff were unable to attend Eddie's funeral in McDonough, Georgia earlier in the summer, but we all had ties to him. The school organized a brief service for our team and welcomed any athletes and students that were already on campus to join us. School wouldn't start for another few days, but nearly everyone on campus came to support us and remember Eddie Gadson's impact on their lives.

Hank Small's empty voice welcomed us to the Chapel. Our salt-and-pepper haired Athletic Director only spoke to the team as a group on a few occasions at the beginning and end of our seasons. Normally when he spoke, his messages were similar and his words were predictable. Today, as he introduced Coach Mills, was different.

As usual, Coach Mills came prepared with a thorough message

For many of us, Eddie's passing didn't seem real until we were reunited with the team; the setting in which we knew him best.

for the attendees. He told Eddie's story as a walk-on and how he earned a scholarship. He spoke of his determination and his work ethic and his commitment to winning at everything he did. Coach Mills flipped through his notes and pushed his fingers through his silver hair. He looked different without his visor. I thought about Eddie and what he'd be like if he were here. He'd be upset with us for all this crying and carrying on. He'd be telling us, "We got work to do!"

Coach Mills continued about family and Eddie's personal impact on his life. He fathered two sons of his own, who often came to practice, but Mills "considered the young men on the team his sons as well, too." The family metaphor had been used on sports teams, even in our locker room. But it had never felt as genuine as it did tonight. I sat next to brothers I was going to inevitably and willingly destroy my body for. Guys who had gone through hell for me and I for them.

Coach Mills wrapped his eulogy to sniffles from across the auditorium. After Mills, Christie Faircloth Dixon, the Student Athlete Success Coordinator, read Paula Gadson's letter to Eddie. Christie's responsibilities as an academic advisor put her in direct contact with athletes and, like the coaches, she cared for us as if we were her own.

Eddie's death never felt real to her. Not until the moment she walked to the front of the auditorium and put her hand on the number 21 jersey draped over the music stand turned podium. She remembered when we received the new jerseys the year before. We pranced around in them like 16-year olds sporting our coolest outfits on the first day of school. She remembered him coming to her office to show off his jersey and how he beamed with pride. That crooked grin stretched ear to ear. As she touched his jersey she realized she would never see him play in it again.

She fought back the tears as she read Paula's letter:

Eddie,

Your Dad always knew you'd be a Boy; even before your birth. He felt that by talking to my belly he was sure to dictate your gender. Of course, that is not how things like that happen, but… I had to admire his ambitious nature. God decided the ultimate outcome the day you were born, but I can't dismiss the possibility of your Dad's influence on his choice! And no matter how it occurred, I would never change the fact that you were, "My Baby Boy…My Pooh Bear." God graced our lives with the wonderful gift of You.

The first time I gazed at you, held you in my arms, and kissed your cheek, I felt the power of a Mother's love. I wanted to protect you, fight for you, and never-ever wanted you to hurt. I couldn't help but squeeze and kiss you a thousand times a day, and though, you at times lightly protested, especially as you matured, because, "that wasn't cool to do in public and in front of your friends", deep down I know, you really enjoyed it.

From your first crooked steps, you let me know our journey together would be filled with happiness. You continuously lifted me up and added such joy to my life. As your wonderful and cheerful personality developed, I admired your ease and confidence. I thought I was supposed to be the one teaching you, but you taught me something new every day. You have genuinely made me a better person.

I know I did not thank you enough for your sacrifice, having to follow Dad and I around while we served in the military. After all, you never asked for the frequent disruptions, absences, and moves. I know it was hard, but you constantly persevered with style. Your spirit and character helped you rise to each impending change and obstacle.

Eddie, you could be hardheaded, (think that came from your Dad), but you had an understanding and protective nature that I was thankful for and valued. I made mistakes along the way, forgive me, but my good intentions were continuously focused on you. Additionally, I want to tell you I am sorry for being the one that, as you put it, "passed on bad genes" and ultimately caused you to be three inches shorter than you thought you should be. I will extremely miss your offhand comments, the jokes, the silly nicknames for Dad and I, and your ability to make me smile even when I wasn't feeling like it. Your smile could light a city.

Most of all, I will miss our conversations. We spoke about anything and everything, even girls. And actually, there were those moments you told me a bit more than I really had wanted to know. But, I am thankful for that, and will forever cherish our relationship, our bond, and our openness.

Eddie, you turned into more of a Man than I ever imagined or hoped you would become. You were a kind and compassionate person that others will forever strive to equal. I am certain you know how VERY PROUD I am of you. And although my wish for our future has been temporarily postponed, and my heart broken, I look forward to the day we reunite.

As you know, it was natural for us to always end a conversation by telling one another how much we cared. So Edward know this, you will always be "Mamma's Baby," you touched my soul, and again, "I Love You."

Forever Your "Psycho," Mom

Coach Barrows was next. His team addresses were typically littered with humor to keep our attention while getting his point across. Today, he was devoid of jokes.

"I am extremely humbled to be before you today," he said, his voice hoarse from the stresses of camp. "I have been asked to read a letter to the team. A letter from Ed Gadson to his son." He made eye contact with everyone in the room, pausing once he laid eyes on Emma, his daughter, sitting a back row. He was a father and he knew what this letter meant to Mr. Gadson. He knew what it would mean to us, the unofficial extension of Eddie's family.

I knew Mr. Gadson, as many of us did. I could picture him in the crowd beaming with delight after his son caught a seemingly impossible ball. I could picture him cheering loudly as his son got up and signaled "first down" with the authority of a referee. His son was a superstar and he had every reason in the world to be proud of his accomplishments. He and Paula had raised a leader of men. We had a duty to honor Ed and Paula through our play. We were hurting, but nowhere near what they had to be going through when he wrote this letter.

Edward... Eddie... Li'l Eddie... My Little Man... Bonehead Number One. I know there is no doubt in your mind that I love you because I made sure you know it in my own special way. I truly treasured the joy you brought into my life during your brief physical time on this earth. You've provided me with enough cherished memories to last two lifetimes. Over the past few days, I've replayed tons of them over and over in my mind. When times get hard and I need a lift, I'll simply recall that bright, cheerful smile of yours and it'll give me the strength to get through whatever's troubling me. I miss you!

I'm not sure how many fathers out there can say they have a son that's truly their friend, but I know I can. I valued our friendship more than any of our other relationships. We were Father and Son, Coach and Player, Teammates, and most of all Friends. Not only were you my friend, but a valuable friend to your mother as well. I don't have to tell you how much she adored you, I would glow inside from the joy she felt every time you did something great, which was quite often. However, I am upset with you for leaving me to have to deal with her on my own. I miss you!!

Eddie, I try my best to be a positive role model for you, but what really ended up happening is that you became a positive role model for me. I couldn't have asked for a better son, even though you often tried my patience, a lot, I mean a lot. I guess you were just fulfilling your role as a son to the T. You didn't want me to wear the title "Daddy" without working for it. I miss you!!!

Our times playing basketball together were one of the greatest joys of my life. I was so excited when you got back into golf because that gave me an excuse to spend even more time with you. I miss you!!!!

As I sat trying to put my thoughts on paper, I was fighting to get the words just right, because it would be my last message to you. But suddenly I realized that was silly because I know we'll still be talking every day for the rest of my life and beyond. I miss you!!!!!

Eddie as I've always told you when things didn't quite go the way you wanted them to, "Everything happens for a reason." Now here I sit trying to make sense out of those same words, concerning you leaving me. I wish there was something I could do to bring you back to me, but the Lord must need you up there with him more than I need you here with me. I keep telling myself that God's football team, the Angels, must have had a losing season last year and he needed an outstanding wide receiver to help get his program back on track. I hope he realizes he's not only getting a top-notch athlete, but he's also getting one heck of a young man that gave and earned respect every day.

I know we'll be reunited someday and your sudden passing will somehow make sense to me then. I'm told that Angels don't age: therefore, you should still be playing football for God's Angels when I join you in heaven. Please reserve me a seat at your games, because you know I'll be at every one of them jumping around and screaming for you like a mad-man. I miss you sooo much!!!!!!

Eddie, I'm crazy about you... You are my "Hero" and definitely, "The Wind Beneath My Wings." Lots of hugs and kisses, Dad.

Coach Barrows finished crying through the letter before he and Jon Davis embraced for a long, tight hug at the foot of the stage. Jon, the campus pastor, wiped his eyes and put his Bible on the stand placed before him. He toggled the height and rubbed his shaved head with his hand. His green eyes weren't fiery and wild like we were used to seeing on Sundays. His eyebrows, which normally sat high and expressed his excitement toward everything, sat flat and focused.

Jon was a former football coach at CSU and an ex-offensive lineman. He lost a few belt notches worth of weight since his playing and coaching days so his sermons regularly included a self-deprecating joke about he and his linemen brethren loving to eat. He defined biblical terms with precision and helped you understand the literal meaning of scripture. He cared about his message and how it was received, today was no exception.

"Today I want to talk about hope," Jon scanned the room with his green eyes. He knew we didn't need jokes or definitions; we needed healing. "First Corinthians 15:50 says, '*I declare to you, brothers and sisters, that flesh and blood cannot inherit the kingdom of God, nor does the perishable inherit the imperishable.*'"

Jon talked about salvation and what God has in store for us and how we can't fathom what He sees. He talked about what Eddie was getting to see right now, in his heavenly form. He talked about Eddie's impact on us and, like Eddie's Mom at the funeral, challenged us to never forget that impact. To live with his passion and to honor our brother in all we did. We all held out as long as possible, but most players and coaches in the room broke down in tears.

The sermon was short, but perfect. Most of us hadn't let the gravity of the situation sink in. Many guys had never given themselves permission to mourn. Jon gave us that permission and he gave us hope.

He gave us comfort, too. "Eddie is in a better place, a place so wonderful and so devoid of pain that we can't imagine what it's like. And he's watching over us from heaven in total comfort," he said as he firmly grasped his bible in his right hand and pointed it to the sky. "Death's sting has been taken away by Jesus and what he did for us on the cross. Let's pray."

Out of the corner of my clouded eye, I could see Reggie wipe his tears and hear him clear his nose. I patted his back as Jon closed in prayer.

I took a quick survey of the Chapel, every cheek in the chapel bore evidence of tears. Even the freshmen, who didn't know Eddie, couldn't help but be touched by the power in the room. For those of us that were in McDonough for the funeral, this was only slightly easier, having gone through this before. This service was no less special, but it was held in the presence of the family that we knew Eddie within. This is how we would always remember him.

Today we mourned the loss of Eddie Gadson. But today was the last time we would do so. When we walked out of the Chapel peace surrounded us. We never discussed it, but we resolved to celebrate his life after that day in the Chapel. The time to mourn had passed and the time to honor him was in front of us.

CHAPTER 16

PRAISES AND PRAYER REQUESTS

SATURDAY, AUGUST 27, 2005

NORTH CHARLESTON, SC

The symphony of practice was music to the coaches' ears. Helmets crashed into each other like cymbals. The bass drum of thumping pads could be heard from every corner of the field. Hot breath whistled like the string section as we tried to communicate with mouthpieces clenched between our teeth.

The practice clock in the corner of the field ticked through the five minute periods. Each interval on the clock matched up perfectly with the practice plans each coach kept in their pocket. We spent no more and no less than the designated time in each drill. Unless of course we didn't perform up to Mills' standards or the defense made the offense look bad. Then he'd just stop the clock until we got it right. The minutes ticked relentlessly, just like a game. Even when Mills paused the clock the pace of practice remained a blur.

"Period 19, 3-on-3!" Coach Mills shouted as the hysteria of the day peaked. "DB's and receivers up first, let's go!"

The last 3-on-3 of camp had begun. We didn't typically beat up on ourselves like this during the season, so this was our last chance to earn bragging rights with our counterparts. I immediately came off the front line of spectators and took the center spot. They stood the same height, they played the same position, and the duo from Charlotte – Jon Carmon and David Misher – flanked me on either side.

Coach Perkins had already pulled CJ to the back spot and was holding on to his jersey, getting him ready for his duties at free safety this season.

As the receivers eyed who was already on the front lines, David, Jon, and I could see them briefly survey who they wanted to challenge. Maurice Price, the emerging stud receiver picked Jon since he was recently named one of the starting corners. Reggie stepped out into his stance and got face to face with David on my right. A freshman named Markus Murry jumped right out and took a spot across from me after fighting off some other receivers for the chance to prove himself. The unexpected lack of depth at receiver meant Markus would be one of two freshmen who may see playing time, he couldn't afford to sit out.

Jon hadn't stopped talking since our numbers were called, "Better get yo weight up, Murry! What are you laughing at, Price? This is gonna be ugly!"

Behind the trio of receivers a "backside as wide as Mercedes Benz," as Coach Kelly put it, that belonged to starting center, Shawn Huntsinger, lined up to snap to Collin Drafts for effect. Shawn would snap it to Collin and he'd hand the ball to a running back before they stood back to watch the action with the rest of the horde. Andre "Dre" Copeland, the transfer from South Florida, was so short I could barely see him standing next to Collin in his running back position. He was almost directly seven yards in front of me. His eyes burned and his two gold teeth were hidden by the mouthpiece he clenched down on.

Like a prison mob eager for a fight, our teammates cheered for us. The winning side of the ball would have to do up-downs as punishment before practice ended. None of us wanted to be the reason the day ended on a bad note. I bumped fists with David and then Jon as we dug our cleats into the ground and sank our butts to out-leverage our opponents. I was so close to Markus I could see the sweat beading off his forehead into his dark brown eyes and on the torn up grass below us.

BEEEP

All six of our helmets instantly collided. The fight had begun. I pumped my feet and got my hands inside of Markus' for leverage. I grabbed the chest piece of his shoulder pads and pressed him away from me. I held the size and strength advantage, weighing a solid twenty pounds more than him, but I knew he wasn't going to give up easily. I wriggled my right hand free and held him off with my left as Dre came barreling toward me. Markus leaned on me a split-second too late, I had Dre in my grasp, driving him into David. David and I combined to push him over the long, blue bags set up as boundaries. We only gave up two of our 10 yards to defend.

"Great job!"

"Second and eight!"

"Atta-boy!"

"Way to finish!"

"Good hands!"

Intensity heightened and the cheers from the defense grew louder and clearer. Someone had rushed over from the defensive sideline to scoop me up by the shoulder pads after the tackle and I was on my feet before I knew it. I helped David up with my right hand and patted his helmet with my left. I didn't bother taking my mouthpiece out, "Good thtuff, leth do it again."

Easier said than done. We lined up at the new spot so close I could see David and Reggie's face masks touching to my right. The whistle blew and I forced Markus backwards, penetrating their front and forcing Dre's momentum to be slowed. Jon and CJ finished him off right around the same yard marker and Coach Mills yelled in his best official's voice, "Third down and seven to go!"

"Come on, fellas," I said through a muffled mouthpiece. "Thwo more; puth 'em back!"

David and I helped our teammates up while the frenzied defensive sideline talked trash to the offense. The next, similar to the first, allowed each of us to hold our ground while CJ wrangled Dre to the ground for only a two-yard gain.

"Good push, finish em!"

"Don't let 'em score!"

The cheers from both sides escalated with every snap. The receivers looked tired, as I'm sure we did. All six of us jumped back to the line of scrimmage and prepared for one last battle.

Markus was able to get a small crease on my left and Jon was too busy fighting with Price to focus on the ball carrier. The drill was set 10 yards wide, but we ended up with a hole the size of a pickup truck that 5'8" Dre could knife through. CJ made impact, but as Coach Kelly constantly reminded us, "He's on scholarship, too," and Dre pushed through the 10-yard marker to score. The offense went nuts as we were consoled by our teammates and the defensive coaches about how, "it's an offensive drill anyways."

"Get your feet choppin'!" Coach Perkins hollered at us as he dug for his whistle in the pocket of his blue coaching shorts.

BEEEP

The buzz of the drill fizzled and exhaustion set in as we finished our prescribed set of 10 up-downs. We were ready to rest.

As practice concluded we came together, as usual, for Coach Mills' calculated recap of announcements, praises, and prayer requests. He typically delivered a predetermined message

incorporating an inspirational quote or scripture for encouragement. In the past, he had referenced everyone from Yogi Berra to
Martin Luther King, Jr. to Jesus in motivational monologues.

"I bet he says something about consistency and how we've
got to keep up this intensity all season. Watch!" Collin had snuck
up behind me and taken a knee next to me in front of Mills. I was
too tired to laugh, but I gave him a smile and a nod to acknowledge
his forecast.

Collin Drafts should have redshirted his first year and watched
from the sideline in his second. That was Mills' original plan,
anyway. His first season the starter went down unexpectedly and
Collin was thrown into the game without a working knowledge of
Mills' complex offense. He didn't know his reads and couldn't remember his progressions. He kept afloat on raw talent, scrambling
around and making just as many plays with his legs as with his arm.

The nerves of his first start, against Presbyterian College,
almost got the best of him. He was so jumpy he nearly peed his
pants before the game. On his third drive, after back-to-back drives
resulting in punts, he was so skittish he bobbled the snap. Mills
knew the freshman was too nervous. The bobbled snap got Collin
benched. After calming down on the sideline for a few plays, he was
given another chance.

"Are you ready to play, or what?" Mills asked him.

Collin responded well to the sharp words from his coach. This
time, another freshman named Eddie, who caught any wild pass
thrown his way, helped the young quarterback find a rhythm.

By the end of the season, though Eddie had been redshirted
with a broken face, Collin matured into more of a quarterback than
Coach Mills expected. Only quicker. His intangibles set him apart
and his competitive flame was impossible to douse. Plus, he bought
into Mills' master plan. He wasn't a neighsayer and he wasn't a rebel
who rejected Mills' authority over the team. He learned the offense
through trial and error his first year. He perfected his knowledge of

Mills' system in his second year with more tools and more time to throw. Going into his third season as the starter, Collin had spent countless hours studying Mills' dink-and-dunk system of short passes and logical adjustments. Many of those hours were spent next to Mills in position meetings or on the field. He spent so much time with Coach Mills he could predict the calls Mills would signal and the critiques he would catch during film. And he could finish Mills' sentences.

"Men," Coach Mills began, "today we showed great intensity from the time we stepped on the field to the time we wrapped up with 3-on-3. We are proud of what you've done this off-season and this preseason as well, too. This will be the best season ever at Charleston Southern University, I have no doubt in my mind." He paused for dramatic effect and the muffled, obligatory applause we gave using our thigh pads. This is the kind of intensity we need to keep throughout the season."

Collin was scary accurate.

After mundane announcements about meetings, laundry, and study hall he moved on to praises and prayer requests: my favorite. These were the nuances that set CSU apart, the little reasons Mom encouraged me to make this my new home. We got the chance to hear teammates' success stories throughout the practice.

Praises were an opportunity for teammates or coaches to stand up in front of the group and publicly acknowledge someone in their position group, someone on the other side of the ball, a coach, or just someone they saw hustling and making plays. This public recognition made us stronger and I loved to hear when we put in hard work. That brought us one step closer to winning more games.

Feelings of hierarchy were non-existent, most of us came in during the same period. As Jim O'Conner put it, "Nobody was out to one-up anyone else."

A vicious, but healthy, competition between the receivers and defensive backs had occurred and we received praise from the other side of the ball. We had gone against each other during one-on-one drills to practice various game-like scenarios. Sometimes we blocked and got off blocks, sometimes we practiced open field tackling, and other times we worked on routes and coverages. Physical contact was unavoidable. We enjoyed this more than the receivers, but they held their own.

We made our presence felt in drills like one-on-ones where they hardly caught any balls and again in the blocking drills where a couple of the receivers had been trampled by the defensive backs on their way to making a tackle. We won most of the competitions that day, but they won the last drill on the "big stage" with everyone watching.

Tempers flared and we pushed each other to improve, a good day of practice if you'd have asked the coaches. Coach Mills mantra for previous years was from Proverbs 27:17 – "*As iron sharpens iron, so does one man sharpen another.*" Today we sharpened each other. The offense needed challenging and we needed to prove ourselves. The spotlight typically beamed brightest on the them.

Our bodies felt like they had been forced through a meat grinder; bruised, cut, and tenderized. The thrill of pushing our bodies to fatigue produced a euphoric feeling that only another athlete could identify. Some athletes train by themselves, we got to do it with 90 of our best friends. We were proud of the receivers, and they of us. We were exhausted from the day's battles, but we carried a sense of accomplishment knowing that both position groups got better that day.

The defensive backs received multiple praises from the receivers as well as the receivers coach, Jamey Chadwell. Coach Chadwell, a native Tennessean whose charisma made him a favorite amongst players, wasn't quick to hand out compliments to the enemy. Behind the Southern charm and the lop-sided smile burned a blazing competitive spirit.

We shot back with praises of our own for guys like our emerging star Maurice Price, the Purdue University transfer Drew

Rucks, and the freshman Markus Murry. Price was the clear leader of the group and he'd taken his share of shots that day, coming out of a tackling drill with screws falling off of his helmet from the collision. Senior defensive back Tavares Shorter, who seemed to deliver big hits only when he felt like making a statement, decleated the 225-pound Rucks in pass skeleton. Rucks, who transferred because the Boilermakers wanted him to play linebacker, ate the hit and jogged back to the huddle with no complaint. Murry witnessed and experienced all of this. He struggled during conditioning earlier in the day, but he seemed to be figuring out his place on the roster. I thought Murry deserved particular praise. In some ways, he reminded us of Eddie.

"I want to praise Markus Murry," I said as I pointed a finger at the freshman. "We did a lot of physical stuff today and he didn't back down from anybody. He's tough and he's going to make a difference this year."

A chorus of "ayyyyyy" and "good job fresh meat" rang out through the massive huddle. I couldn't tell if he was blushing or just exhausted, but he shot me a "thank you" head nod.

After all the praises were awarded, we moved on to prayer requests. Some of the team asked for prayers for family members going through illnesses. Others thoughtfully sent up prayer requests for injured teammates like Josh Warrior who was healing from a broken back.

Unspoken prayer requests were common at the end of practice. A group of 90 teammates can be intimidating to a young man that may be struggling with some personal issues. A raise of the hand and a nod of the head was all it took for someone to signal they didn't have anything to share, but that they needed some prayers to go their way.

Sometimes Coach Mills prayed and occasionally one of my teammates prayed, but most of the time assistant coaches would step up to the plate. In his thick Tennessee twang, Coach Chadwell went through the specific prayer requests with perfect recollection, detailing ones he knew more about from private conversations. He talked about how Eddie would be proud of how we worked in this heat and how he's watching over us. Then he made a catch-all for the unspoken prayer requests to be sure they were not forgotten. As he wrapped up, Coach Chadwell thanked God for us, the team. In his own way he praised every one of us for a hard day of work.

Weary, but proud, we marched off the practice field. We got better.

CHAPTER 17

TYING TIES

SUNDAY, AUGUST 28, 2005

NORTH CHARLESTON, SC

Each Sunday since camp began we had gone to church as a team. We toured this circuit every year during preseason. Charleston, South Carolina is nestled comfortably in the Bible Belt where the only thing that outnumbers churches are palmetto trees. The coaches used this fact to our advantage. Each Sunday we would visit a different church. We sampled Baptist Churches, Methodist churches, and other non-denominational churches. Churches where the only black people in the room came with us and Historically Black Churches as well. Some services were less than an hour and some went on long after 90 of us snuck out the side door because church was going to wreck our practice schedule.

I had a theory that we went to so many churches to raise community awareness that Charleston Southern University had a football team. Most people didn't care about any football outside of their half of the Clemson/South Carolina rivalry so we took advantage of the face time with new crowds. Though we hadn't done anything noteworthy yet, it was fun to have everyone applaud when they announced our presence. It was a good strategy, some of the congregations totaled more than the fans at our home games.

Though some of the guys vehemently opposed going to church – I could never figure out why, CSU never hid behind the fact that it was a faith-based university – I enjoyed it. I grew up in the church and I knew I could use a sprinkle of "good influence" outside of the coaches. Today, on the last Sunday before classes resumed, we would visit Summerville Baptist Church a few miles up the road.

CJ and I got dressed early on the Sundays we attended church as a team. We seldom passed up an opportunity to put on a tie or make an impression; we never knew who we were going to see in church. We were also two of eight guys on the team who could tie our own ties. This meant a line of muscular necks would soon be forming outside of our dorm room with ties in hand.

The Quads were large, hollow, cinder-block square structures with an open grassy area in the center. Everyone's rooms faced inward and as the sun was peaking more and more over the eastern side, we could see more doors start to open up. We couldn't leave the door open or we would sweat through our church clothes in 12 seconds, flat. Instead, we opened the blinds on the large window next to the door to let the rest of the team know we were "open for business."

"Hey Juice, can you tie this thing for me?" called David Misher as our first customer walked into the room with his tie dangling around his neck. CJ, responding to the term of endearment, stopped fidgeting with his own tie and focused on David's as I finished lacing up my dress shoes. Bobby Adams staggered in behind David struggling with his own tie and looking as lost as puppy without a collar.

Some of the older guys, like David and Bobby, knew we would tie their ties for them so they came strolling up casually. Others would rush around banging on a few guys' doors before someone sent them to us in a panic. It seemed as though we had everyone covered for the day. Caravans of cars were being filled in the parking lot outside of the Quads when I spotted the tie Okeba Rollinson had hanging halfway to his knees.

"Hey, Okeba," I hollered as he walked toward the parking lot, "come here, let me fix your tie. You look sloppy."

"No I don't!" he said slapping at my hands as they reached for the white collared shirt that contrasted against his black skin.

"Come on man, you look like a fourth grader who borrowed your dad's tie. It's not supposed to go down past your belt like that."

"Oh it isn't? Okay, can you fix it real quick?" he asked, changing his tune once he realized I was looking out for him instead of making fun of him. He jutted his sparsely whiskered chin to the sky and stood still long enough for me to adjust the brown paisley material to the proper height.

Though Okeba and I previously had a friendly relationship, we had gotten to know each other better since camp started. He was Tavares Shorter's and my backup and we had spent time together going over the defensive schemes. I felt comfortable around him, as I did everyone else on the team.

I finished Okeba's tie, told him he looked sharp, and gave him an "atta-boy" on the butt for encouragement. This was normally something we did while in pads, but as we spent so much time together, nobody cared. In pads, out of pads, it's all the same. It wasn't unusual to see the same display of affection at a party or in between classes. Little could be done to embarrass each other, even in public.

We shared some of our most physically and mentally trying times together, helping push and pull each other through them. The most stone-cold guy on the planet had a sense of camaraderie with his teammates after camp concluded. It didn't matter what color you were, where you were from, or what position you played. We all knew the struggles each other had been through, which strengthened our bonds. Finishing camp was an accomplishment in itself.

Coach Kelly, the offensive line coach, "preached" servant leadership. His words about serving stuck in my head like a song on repeat. Anything I could do to serve my teammates, I would do it. Most of the time it was motivation and encouragement on the field. Sometimes it was helping with schoolwork, but other times it was tying a tie. Egos didn't have a place on the team. We were all in it together. We'd need every ounce of that strength banded together to beat The Citadel in six days.

Team Roster

1 – Maurice Price
2– Jonna Lee
3 – Anthony Lewis
4 – Dimar Labega
5 – Justin Williams
6 – Tavares Shorter
7 – Collin Drafts
8 – Anthony Moore
9 – Drew Rucks
10 – Eli Byrd
11 – Bryan Meers
13 – Nick Ellis
14 – Bryant Burch
15 – Sidney Bryant
17 – Markus Murry
18 – Dennis Delemar
19 – Terrence Scurry
20 – Craig Washington
21 – Eddie Gadson
22 – CJ Hirschman
23 – Antione Thomas
24 – Daniel Williams
25 – John Compton
26 – Marvin McHellon
27 – Jonathan Carmon
28 – Andre Copeland
29 – Okeba Rollinson
30 – David Misher
32 – Kenny Harper
33 – Emmate Epps
34 – Reggie Ellington
35 – Mike McCann
36 – Chase Chambers
38 – Ishmael Gordon
39 – Matt Durham
40 – Kevin Mitchell
41 – Alexius Ferguson
42 – Caleb Geiger
43 – Jim O'Connor
44 – Robert Adams
45 – Juwon Lawson

46 – Darius Jackson
47 – Hart Pearson
48 – Stonewall Randolph III
50 – Maurice Sellers
51 – Josh Mitchell
52 – Travis Jefferson
53 – George Shaw
54 – Jada Ross
55 – Eric Justice
56 – Jarrett Johns
57 – Foster Moore
58 – Shawn Huntsinger
60 – Rick Howell
61 – Carl Kramer
62 – Mark Wise
63 – DeAndre Harrison
64 – Alex Bragg
65 – Adam Degraffenreid
66 – Donald Fondren
68 – Brandon Stoudemire
69 – Frank Gil
70 – Matt Hoisington
71 – JW Myers
72 – Wes Houston
73 – Devin Maffett
74 – Troy James
75 – Josh Gravely
76 – David Bishop
79 – Charlie Byars
80 – Edsel Logan
81 – Kevin Clabaugh
82 – Clayton Coffman
83 – Robert Rivers
84 – Ricky Taylor
86 – Ryan Robertson
88 – Kelby Taylor
89 – Brian Palm
90 – Christian D'Agostino
91 – Mike McCoy
92 – Phil Jordan
93 – Ryan Ard
95 – Brandon Horton

96 – Brett Bowdren
97 – Zach Barton
98 – Alex Thomas
99 – Tyrese Harris

Practice Squad/IR

Josh Warrior
Jovan Kirksey
Brent Dennison
Randy Bosart
Terrance Reese
Chris Harris
Robert Whitney
Bert Wright
Leonard Davis
Blake Dyar
Antione Freeman
Matt Hurd
Chris Miller
John McClelland
Tyler Morse
Raymond Glover
Chris Guisti
Timothy Henderson

Coaches

Jay Mills
Steve Barrows
Darrell Perkins
Chris Achuff
Chuck Kelly
Scott Browne
Jamey Chadwell

Assistants

Fred Gambrell
Jonathan Parra
Ben Ballenger
Tom Slade
Darren Swigget

CHAPTER 18

THE CITADEL

FRIDAY, SEPTEMBER 2, 2005

CHARLESTON, SC

We entered the first week of the season anxious to play the first game. It was a nerve-racking feeling knowing that we had worked since November of the previous year, every day, and we were finally going to be tested.

The first game of the season is your first true test as a team. Everything else can be deceiving and nothing in the world can simulate the magnitude of a college football game. Scrimmages aren't always accurate and you don't know how well you're conditioned until you meet another team for four full quarters. Most of all, you don't know who's going to perform when the game is on the line.

It's true that you learn a lot from winning, but you learn more from losing. We thought we'd been taught enough lessons from the five losses we suffered in 2004. We were ready to start winning games. We thought ourselves a championship-caliber team and were ready to prove it to the Citadel Bulldogs in less than 24 hours. We lacked a storied rivalry and they didn't even consider us a blip on their big-time Southern Conference radar. They were more concerned with in-conference opponents like the National Champion contending Appalachian State Mountaineers. Nonetheless, we had marked this day on the calendar. Aside from our in-conference opponents like Coastal Carolina and Gardner Webb, this could prove to be the biggest game of our year. They had embarrassed us by 34 points in 2002 and again by 54 points in 2003. In 2004, a year they only won three games, they opted not to play us after a hurricane forced us to reschedule. We had become a legitimate threat and, as we saw it, they were scared to add another loss to their schedule.

Coach Barrows challenged us to be the championship-caliber team that could beat a Southern Conference team during his speech to the defense the day before the game.

"Men, we have endured a lot over the past nine months. Coach Perk, Achuff, and the rest of the coaches, we're proud of all you've overcome. But tomorrow is our first true test."

He always seemed to be hoarse and he was talking low, but in a calm tone. His silvering, brown hair looked clean and his voice sounded like his throat had been polished with sandpaper as he talked about our performance.

I zoned out while he droned on about our schemes and duties. I knew my job like the back of my hand; I had studied harder for this game than I did for my SAT's. But something was weird. I was nervous. This was only my second start and it happened to come during the biggest game I'd ever been a part of. Tomorrow would be my chance to make a name for myself, my chance to make a major contribution. Sure, I had played in all but a single game last year and made 13 tackles in my debut against Coastal in the last game of the season. But this was different.

"Men, I want to challenge you to finish the game," Barrows said. "To believe we can win it. I know we think we can win it, but it takes more than that. We haven't finished many games except VMI last year. Focus on your assignments for four quarters and let's start this season the right way. Degraf, break us down."

Adam Degraffenreid put a clenched fist in the air and scanned the room to make sure everyone was doing the same. "Let's do it tomorrow. Make a statement. 'D' on two. One... Two...

"D!"

As we re-arranged the meeting room to accommodate the offensive unit behind the adjacent curtain, Darius Jackson stood up on a chair. He signaled for our attention with his long fingers from above the crowd.

"Hey fellas. We all know what this game means so I don't need to tell y'all how to get up for it. But I... I did want to share this." His voice cracked and emotion preoccupied his dark brown eyes. This impromptu speech had to be important, Darius wasn't one to stand up before the group. "Eddie hated 'dem Citadel boys. All he wanted was to beat 'em. In case y'all need some extra motivation, think about Eddie looking down on us tomorrow." Determination that bordered on anger consumed his face. The same kind of passion Eddie would have displayed on an afternoon like this.

His simple and powerful words were exactly what we needed to hear.

– – – *Saturday, September 3, 2005* – – –

The air was thick and muggy as we walked onto the field. My gold pants fit comfortably tight, like a boxer's gloves before he steps into the ring. The straps of my shoulder pads pressed against my ribs, slipping and sliding with the lubrication of my sweat. On top of the pads, my baggy jersey refused to stay tucked. My helmet pressed against my temples and my chinstrap pulled snug, though slippery, from the perspiration collecting in it. Behind the face mask, my mind prepared for what was about to happen next.

"If the tight end crashes down, expect a pulling guard followed by the Tailback..." My internal dialogue was precise. "If they option for some reason, take the pitch man... If it's a three step drop back, look for the quick slant… Be sure Okeba knows the plays, he's starting in place of Tavares…"

I gazed across the sideline and saw the Bulldogs slapping each other's helmets and pumping each other up. My mind raced with images of what they would do and how we could crush them in varying situations. I hoped we would catch them dragging a receiver across the middle, I just wanted one shot at him.

"Kickoff Team get ready!" Coach Barrows stood next to me. "Let's get this thing ready, McCann!" he said as we hustled to the pre-labeled Special Teams mat halfway between the offensive and defensive benches. "We practiced this and practiced it. You guys know what to do; it's time to prove yourselves to this crowd! Deep left. Deep left. Hit on three! One… Two… Three…"

We shouted, "HIT!" in unison and trotted toward the 40-yard line. I found my spot, just inside the hash-mark and set my feet wide so I could sink my butt and get ready for an all out sprint. I faced our sideline and looked past the kicker to see the rest of my team lined up on the sideline. Every one of them had their helmets raised to the pinkish-blue South Carolina sky. We were ready for a fight. Some were screaming and pumping their fists in the air. Some were calm and focused. I could feel their energy all the way across the field!

A long, loud whistle ensued and I closed my eyes for a split second to remind myself what I was here for, "Hit somebody."

The kicker's hand went up and we began trotting toward the line of scrimmage, picking up speed as we closed the gap. The thud of the kick to my left signaled that we should already be in a full sprint. Check.

I gave a quick move to the front line blocker that tried to get his hands on me before a back line blocker got in my path. I gave two quick steps, lowered my hips and squared up with him, putting my facemask into his sternum and immediately extending my arms to create separation and keep the ball to my left. As soon as I spotted the ball carrier going toward our sideline, I shucked the Bulldog and sprinted to help finish off the play. Marvin McHellon and Jim O'Connor combined for a crushing tackle in front of the defensive bench that had sent the sideline into a frenzied celebration by the time I was able to join in.

"Good hit baby! Good hit!" Was all I could muster after that sprint. I turned and walked backwards onto the field, welcoming each of my defensive teammates with low fives. Behind my helmet, my eyes scanned the sideline for Coach Barrows. His blue hat popped through the crowd of energetic faces with hands waving in the air like he was erasing a chalkboard. "Base Garnet!" I repeated as soon as he could get through the whole sequence. "Base Garnet Mish!" I shouted as David signaled that he'd received the call with a thumb's up.

I shifted my focus to the tight end in front of me and crept into position. Five yards deep, three yards from the end man on the line of scrimmage. Where are the tight end's eyes? Does the offensive line have their weight on their hands or on their feet?

"Hut!"

I took a small step forward as the ball was snapped, mirroring the tight end. "Run! Run!" I yelled as soon as I recognized the play. I could see the pulling guard coming my way and the tight end coming out to block me. I stepped into the blocker with my right shoulder and shrunk the hole as best I could for Josh Mitchell, our middle linebacker to fill. I couldn't see much due to the tight end laying over my shoulder, but I could hear the collision Josh made with the guard. Josh and I played in high school together and I knew he rarely lost those battles. The slamming of helmets sounded like gunfire and I knew Josh won his battle. The running back spilled out behind the tight end who was blocking me as I saw Josh chasing him from the inside out. I pulled the tight end's jersey downward and took a step back, pulling him to the ground as I corralled the running back between Josh and me. The tailback crunched beneath us and we tackled him with ease. CJ, who had joined in on the fun at some point without me noticing, helped push the three of us backwards for a loss of one. Great start!

"Whoooooo!" Josh and I screamed as we congratulated each other and jogged back to our side of the ball.

"Second 'n 'leven, good start boys! Keep it going!" My voice, though loud, was muffled by the rubber mouthpiece I chewed on. I scanned the sideline for Coach Barrows. "Do it again," I shouted.

A penalty pushed the Bulldogs back five yards before Duran Lawson, the Citadel quarterback, completed a four yard pass; hardly enough for a first down. CJ broke up Lawson's next pass and the defense traded places with the punt return team.

We started a typical "young team's game" by coming out white-hot with enthusiasm like a runner who sprints the first mile of a marathon. We set the tone of the game with our physical play on defense but only two minutes had run from the game clock, there was more football to be played. We traded short drives but The Citadel scored first. They snatched a 7-0 lead with 5:07 left in the first quarter after assembling a near flawless 66-yard drive.

10,361 fans, more than the number that attended all of our home games combined from the year prior, filled the newly renovated stands of Johnson Hagood Stadium to watch what they hoped would be a blowout. Their alumni base came out in droves while their uniformed "Knobs," freshman cadets, packed the bleachers behind our bench. Their white shirts and gray pants formed a sea of screaming hecklers set only 10 feet from us.

The offense struggled for the remainder of the first half and we did what we could on defense to get off the field and give them more opportunities. Neither team could find the endzone before halftime and we entered the third quarter still down by a touchdown, 7-0, Citadel. We deferred at the beginning of the game, a classic Coach Mills decision, so we would receive this half.

Collin and the offense racked up three first downs and capped the first drive of the second half with a touchdown, 7-6, Citadel.

The Citadel's second drive ended in a touchdown
as a majority of the defense helplessly watched.

For only the second time in history the Charleston Southern Buccaneers were about to be tied with the mighty Citadel Bulldogs from across town. The momentum the drive provided could be felt by everyone in the stadium. The better we played, the louder they roared.

I removed my gloves and turned to Nick Ellis to offer him my bare fist along with words of encouragement for his first performance of the year, "Make it seven." Our long snapper got the ball to me perfectly, I pulled it down and tilted it ever so slightly toward Nick. He struck the ball smoothly with his right foot. On point, as usual: 7-7.

The Citadel let us know they were ready to take back the momentum with a few strong running plays on the ensuing drive. I was on the opposite side of the field, wrestling with a would-be blocker, when I saw the third play of the series going away from me. I gripped the chest plate of the blocker's shoulder pads and shed him from my path to the ball carrier.

One of the reasons I enjoyed playing time early in my career was because I understood what the coaches wanted. And more importantly, why they wanted it. They believed the harder you worked on the field, the more opportunities you create for the team. Hard work, on the field, translates to hustling "through the whistle," as Coach Perk put it. I learned early in my football career that hustle always paid off.

Though the tackle was already being made, I arrived on the scene right as the ball squirted out of Lawson's grip. I dove at the ball as it bumbled around like a greased up watermelon heading on a crooked path for the sideline. I recovered the fumble at their 35-yard line to put us in scoring position. Had I not been sprinting to the ball, it would have bounced out of bounds and the Bulldogs would have kept possession. My hard work paid off and now we had an opportunity to take the lead with excellent field position.

The Buccaneer offense, plagued by penalties, struggled against the Citadel's defense during the first half.

Maurice Price (1) catches a deep pass and sprints for a 38-yard gain.

Coach Mills didn't waste any time play-calling and we led the Citadel for the first time in history, 14-7. We could feel the momentum at our backs, we had finally started to get familiar with the feeling. Tension loosened and grins came easier. We made the plays we were supposed to make and The Citadel seemed to trip over their own feet. We let ourselves think we could really pull out a victory.

We traded field position once again before Lawson made up for the fumble with a drive comprised of five consecutive completions that spanned two minutes and 75 yards. The game was tied going into the fourth quarter.

All of the off-season work, all of the 5:30 a.m. workouts, all of the pain and torture of camp, all of the training had been preparing us for this. The fight had been even all night, neither team obtaining a major lead at any point. We had never beat them and just two years prior they embarrassed us 64-10, scoring from the five yard line in the last minutes of the game instead of taking a knee to waste the remainder of the clock. Nothing would satisfy our desire for revenge more than beating the Bulldogs on their field in front of their crowd. One quarter left.

The Citadel had been here before. They regularly competed with teams like Georgia Southern and Wofford and Furman. They knew how to close games out and they knew what they needed to do to send us back across town with disappointment.

12:23 left in the game, touchdown Citadel. We had to answer. Collin and the offense took the field with a swagger we hadn't seen before. Their positive attitudes and their eagerness to take the field gave us hope. The score was still close, all we needed was one touchdown to tie the game up. Maybe Mills would go for two and we'd win with a single score. Maybe Nick would have to kick the game winner for us. Revenge would be ours.

One of the best things about sports is the ability to lose one's self in the game and go to a place where personal struggles don't exist. Where family or relationship issues don't bog us down. Where

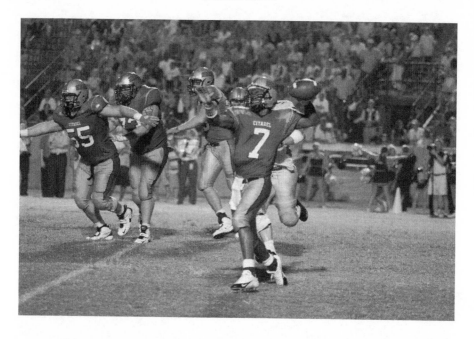

Citadel Bulldog quarterback Duran Lawson (7) cocks and launches a pass downfield while being chased by Buccaneer defensive end Mikey McCoy (91).

all of our cares seem to drain from our bodies through our sweat glands. No time to think about life, only time to think about the task at hand and the reaction needed. If you've trained hard enough, your reactions are the right ones that lead to victory.

We started slow: Stuffed for no gain. Sacked for a loss of seven. Completion for 20. Picked off and returned 46 yards to our eight-yard line. The Bulldogs scored again within three minutes of their last touchdown. To us, the momentum was a horse that hadn't been broken, we tried to hold on but it bucked us off and left us bruised. The Citadel had been here before and they knew how to handle themselves. We, on the other sideline, had only successfully completed one comeback.

Between the screaming Knobs and the white paint of the sideline, heads dropped and helmets were thrown aimlessly. The interception didn't have to be final, but we weren't mentally prepared to come back from it. We lost focus and got ahead of ourselves. As a young team, we understood needing to overcome deficits and staying focused on winning the game, but we didn't know what that felt like. Resolve, like our hardened muscles, needed to be exercised in order to be strong. That day we learned what it meant to finish a game. Unfortunately, we learned it by watching The Citadel finish what they started. They didn't play for revenge, but for each other.

We didn't rack up a ton of yards on the ground, but then again that was not our game. We excelled through the air with the Preseason Conference Co-Player of the Year, Collin Drafts throwing mostly to Maurice Price. Drafts threw for 243 yards, completing 21 of 32 passes with a touchdown. Price caught seven of those passes for 112 yards.

Our defense played well enough to hold The Bulldogs to 14 points through three quarters. Our linebacking corps, affectionately labeled the Band of Brothers by their position coach, Barrows, played the game like wild animals. The three starting Band of Brothers had raked in 28 tackles while 19 other defenders tallied 31 tackles.

"This sucks," I said under my breath as I sat shirtless in the visiting locker room. My body still seeped sweat, though we hadn't been active for nearly 30 minutes. I could feel the onset of soreness in every muscle.

"I know man," CJ said softly as he wrestled to remove his clothes. "We should have beat them. They weren't better than us, we just didn't finish," he stood to put his socks in the respective laundry pile. "They're one of the best teams on our schedule, and they're in the SoCon. We were that close. At least we know we can hang."

"Yeah and now it looks like they blew us out with those last two touchdowns." I unraveled my wrist tape and peeled the sticky pre-wrap from my body. "28-14 isn't a great way to start a winning season."

We had been humbled, but we were excited to know that we could compete with what we considered a legitimate 1-AA

Quarterback Collin Drafts (7), led by fullback Jim O'Connor (43), dives into the endzone for our last score of the game before The Citadel recorded three unanswered touchdowns to solidify their victory.

team that played in a competitive conference. Disappointment rather than anger permeated the locker room. The perfect season we had hoped to dedicate to Eddie and the Gadson family was no longer attainable. But The Citadel wasn't in our conference and technically this loss didn't make a difference in the conference standings. Besides, nobody other than the people in our locker room expected us to win this game anyway.

We knew we could have, and should have, played a better game. The loss frustrated us, but we didn't see the need to change anything we'd been doing. We performed good enough, or so we told ourselves, we just had to learn to finish.

To view more images from the Citadel game, go to http://BelieveEG21.com/citadel

CHAPTER 19

PRESBYTERIAN COLLEGE

FRIDAY, SEPTEMBER, 9, 2005

NORTH CHARLESTON, SC

The loss didn't stress us out. The fact that the Citadel appeared to dominate the box score didn't even annoy us. We were disappointed in how we played. Coach Mills, and countless other coaches, lecture on the subject of winning games versus losing them. Most games, as they explain, are lost through mistakes or a lack of focus. A team is rarely downright "beat" by the other. Due to the high number of losses over the past two seasons, it was one of Coach Mills' favorite subjects. As he put it, we lost the game to The Citadel, they didn't beat us.

Football, like many competitions, requires a certain amount of arrogance to win. It doesn't always have to be apparent to the rest of the world, but it needs to be in your mind. I like to think of it as "cocky on the inside, confident on the out." If the team doesn't wholeheartedly believe it can win before kickoff, it won't.

So we'd tell ourselves, even after a loss, we played well. We'd tell ourselves that we gave it away. That we could have won it if we gave it our all. This same arrogance is what gives us the confidence to "know" that in the next game we will show up and dominate like we should have the week before. It's this arrogance that can help drag teams out of losing streaks. Or it can be the reason Goliath falls to David.

"How you feelin' 'bout tomorrow, dude?" I asked my suite-mate Josh Mitchell as I entered his half of the dorm suite through the conjoined bathroom.

He looked up from his computer as I settled down backwards in the desk chair across from him. In another lifetime Josh Mitchell would have been a Viking. Standing 6'2" with white-blonde hair and blue eyes, he was the prototypical Norseman. And when he stepped onto the field, he acted like one; crashing into offensive lineman and running backs without hesitation.

He stared at the beige cinder block walls for a minute before making eye contact with me. "Great. We had a strong week of practice. Everyone was flyin' around, making plays all week. And they don't run a complicated offense, it's just like ours."

"I know, right, easy for us," I answered with a nod. "They just don't seem that good. And we've almost beat two of the best teams we've played in the past two years, Coastal and The Citadel. We're gonna crush those Hose!"

We shared a laugh as CJ walked in the air conditioned room. He flung his backpack on his bed and joined in the conversation.

"What's so funny?" he asked with his mischievous grin.

"We're playing the Presbyterian 'Blue Hose,' that's what's funny." I smiled wide and made eye contact with him as he plopped into his bed. "I feel like I'm going to laugh every time they announce 'Hose' over the loudspeaker tomorrow. I'll always think that's funny."

"Yeah, and you know what?" he asked as he pointed at the two of us. "It's gonna be even funnier when we're stomping them!"

"I know," I said as I turned the chair around, "we're gonna crush 'em! Coach Perk seems to think they're better than we do. I mean, I've been watchin' film all week and they don't impress me. Nothin' they do is different from our offense and we see that every day. They're not that big! But all the coaches keep tellin' us they're better than we think."

"Barrows was the same way all week," Josh agreed about his own position coach and hunched back down into his laptop. "Whatever..."

"Hey, this is our coming out game," said CJ enthusiastically, "we're gonna destroy them and then start a 10-game winning streak!"

– – – *Saturday, September 10, 2005* – – –

I had hardly spoken a word to anyone since I woke up four hours earlier. I could see the sun at intermittent spurts every time the double locker room doors swung open. "Hot," is all I could think of. In the sanctuary of the locker room the heat couldn't get to us. Outside the double doors the oven cranked to 90 with the humidity turned on full blast.

An anonymous coach hollered "Specialists in five minutes!"

Everyone prepared for the game differently. Butterflies slammed into the walls of my belly at 1,000 miles per hour. Some guys quietly concentrated on their assignments. Some guys were louder and loose. Some guys were nervous. Some puked. Most, like me, blared headphones so we could drown out anything but our own thoughts. Today, Rage Against The Machine's "Live At The Grand Olympic Auditorium" reverberated in my eardrums. Outside of my headphones the locker room rustled with last minute preparation.

Pre-game preparation was not time for jokes. It was not a time to talk about girls or what's happening after the game. It was time to do one thing: get ready to make plays. When we got to the field we could loosen our grip, but not now. Not yet.

Football is a demanding sport. It demands full attention. It demands relentless effort. And it demands a willingness to push through physical pains. To put ourselves in the mindset to win football games we had to take ourselves to another place. A place every man had to get to on his own. Like a gas leak, anticipation silently filled the room. We were cautious not to get too excited in the locker room, we didn't want to spark the fire too early. That's what kickoff was for.

"Specialists! Let's go!" said Coach Perkins through the double doors.

I stood up and stuffed my gloves into the front of my pants. I strapped my helmet and opened my jaw wide to loosen it up before walking to the double doors.

"You ready to do this, buddy?" I felt an open palm give me a few taps on the helmet as I turned to meet Nick Ellis' helmet staring up at mine.

"Yeah man, how 'bout you?" I returned the pat on the helmet as we walked through the double doors, beginning our journey to the game field via the long, worn path that passed the pond.

As we walked side by side toward the field, I rushed through their plays in my mind. "Bubble comes in Trey, not Trio. Don't get sucked in by play action. They run trick plays, stay home."

An instrumental version of T.I's "Bring Em Out" played over the speakers to an audience of athletic trainers and school employees preparing the stadium for the day's event.

We met Coach Perkins and Coach Barrows in the southeast corner of the endzone. I focused my eyes on our new scoreboard. "Charleston Southern" was written in blue letters set to a white background across the top. The small video section in the center rotated starting player's profiles. "CSU - 0" on the left, "PC - 0" on the right.

As Nick and I led the Specialists, jogging around the far endzone into our stretch lines, I could see something on the far end of the field. Coach Barrows had taken the liberty of painting a large black dot on the field with the inscription "EG21" to match the sticker on our helmets. His way of honoring Mr. and Mrs. Gadson before the game.

The circle was nearly 10 feet in diameter and strategically placed on the 21-yard line, indicative of Eddie's number 21 jersey. My eyes locked on the dot to my left as we trotted down the side-line. I couldn't help but give Nick another pat on the helmet as we passed it, sensing where his eyes and his mind were in that moment. He missed Eddie. Not even his game face could cover that up.

To the right stood the Buccaneer stadium and all its mediocrity. A four-story, cream-colored structure known as the Whitfield Stadium Center stood behind the middle section of bleachers. Below the third floor windows, which had slowly begun to fill up with the president's guests, "BUCCANEERS" was printed on the building in bold blue letters. Just below the blue letters sat a dozen or so rows of blue folding seats reserved for Buc Club members and their guests. The blue seats were tucked behind and in between another 20 rows of metal, backless bleachers. The Stadium Center was flanked on either side by a smaller section of metal bleachers mostly reserved for the band and the few dozen students comprising the Buc Wild club.

The sun burned overhead, the air was thick, and the field steamed like a swamp. We didn't know any other kind of football besides this. CJ's words from last night rang in my head, "our coming out game." This is it, this is when our season starts – our first home game of the season. Through warm-ups all I could think about was our first win and what the atmosphere was going to be like when we walked off the field. We'd greet family and friends after the game with smiles and sweaty jerseys. We'd sing the alma mater and walk proudly off the field. We'd meet for food in the parking lot with parents and we'd go out downtown later that night. Today was gonna be great.

The Presbyterian Blue Hose came out of the locker room flat, almost like they were tired and didn't want to be here. We, on the other hand, hollered and executed warmups excitedly in anticipation our first win of the season. We knew the Blue Hose were not going to roll over for us. In fact, we had lost to PC 12 times in a row. But this was a new year and a new team.

We deferred, as always, until the second half. As soon as The Blue Hose got their hands on the ball, they made it known that they were here to play. They picked up first down after first down, completing passes and gaining hard rushing yards on every play. They compiled a 12 play, 80 yard drive finishing with a touchdown after only 3:04 of play. We had been stunned, like the bully who picked on the wrong kid in class.

Offense did what they could to move the ball, but PC wasn't having much of it. Dre Copeland took four handoffs to get the ball moving, but we fell apart once they started getting pressure on us. The Blue Hose defense, just like us, had practiced against a familiar offense for weeks. Nothing we tried was new to them and they anticipated everything we did. Their game plan was flawless and we were forced to attempt a 51-yard field goal – a distance Nick had only made during practice. The kick fell short and PC picked up where they left off the previous drive.

I watched from the sideline as I saw a bubble screen develop, a play that we saw every single day against our own offense. "The bubble" was CSU's offensive bread and butter and we knew exactly how to stop it. The inside slot receiver Chris Pope, who I'd studied for hours over the past week, took a big step back and bowed his route toward the sideline. He'd probably catch the ball, the play has a high completion percentage. As long as we limited his yards-after-catch, YAC for short, the play should end quickly.

"Bubble! Bubble! The bubble is coming! No YAC!" I screamed and jumped and did anything I could to alert the guys on the field. "Stay outside! Here it comes!"

The bubble screen is a quick pass to a two or three receiver side where the outside receiver blocks down and the inside receiver "bubbles" behind the line of scrimmage to try and get outside of the blocking receiver. The corner has to stay outside of the blocking receiver and the safety has to fill the gap by running to the ball inside out. If either misses their responsibility, Pope could be gone down the sideline.

We knew how to stop it. We knew what to do. But we didn't do it. The quick bubble screen turned into a 60-yard play when we should have stopped it for a loss. We weren't on our game. We didn't hustle to get around blocks. We didn't pursue to meet the receiver at the right angle. Some guys stopped chasing once Pope passed them by a couple yards. I watched from the sideline as more than one teammate gave up pursuing the play from behind.

"What are you doing? Finish the play!" I screamed with fury, knowing he could be caught. "Keep chasing him! This drive isn't over yet!"

Quitting on a play was unacceptable. I, and countless others on the sideline, was let down by the guys who stopped chasing Pope. He wasn't exceptionally fast or overly talented, but we just made him look like an NFL prospect. I knew I could have stopped the play if I was in the game. I glared at Coach Barrows for not having me in the game. Though I technically started the game, we had adjusted our game plan to better suit PC's offense. Not an awesome decision, so far.

Marvin McHellon had done his job and turned Pope inside, not letting him have access to the outside lane. After he did his job near the sideline, he sprinted upfield and caught Pope at our five-yard line. Though his efforts technically saved a touchdown, it didn't matter. PC stepped into the endzone after only two plays.

Body language tells all. Because faces are hidden, we naturally became adept at reading each other's body signals and quirks. On the football field, I could tell two players apart without ever seeing a face or reading a number. Someone's jog or stance revealed more about their attitude than anything they could be saying behind their facemask. After the first touchdown we looked like a kid on the playground who just had his toys stolen by the class bully.

The first quarter ended with the Blue Hose on top by two touchdowns, though it felt worse. We talked through what was happening on the field on the defensive bench while the offense sputtered through another sloppy drive. Coach Barrows pointed fingers and asked questions, making sure we all knew what to do. Knowledge wasn't what we lacked. We were all frustrated and PC seemed to be completing everything. They hardly went backwards and they didn't make mistakes. They grabbed small chunks of field and slowly demoralized us with each drive.

Personally, I was frustrated because we were in a new defense that didn't involve me. We put another lineman in the game and took out a defensive back to give ourselves more run support. It wasn't working and I knew I could make a difference, just like the bubble play. I had been stuck watching from the sideline for most of the game thus far.

We traded short drives as the second quarter drug on. They moved the ball consistently and if they didn't score, they pinned us inside our own 20 yard line with calculated punts. We filled the second quarter with mental mistakes like missed blocks and penalties; exactly the kind of play that drives men like Coach Kelly to put his fist through a marker board. The harder we tried to concentrate, the more we misstepped. Dropped passes and missed tackles littered the field worse than the Canada Goose poop on the practice field.

By halftime we trailed 21-0. Bodies collapsed like rag dolls in the lockers, exasperated from the beating we were enduring. Faces and arms, the only exposed skin, flushed red and sweat gushed from our pores. We sulked in pools of our own sweat, more dejected than ever.

The locker room was no longer loud and boisterous as in pregame. We were quiet and embarrassed. Coach Barrows and Coach Perkins, sensing our lack of enthusiasm, made some adjustments

and did what they could to give us a new sense of spirit. Coach
Mills' speech was dry and uninspiring. He could have been Win-
ston Churchill delivering his "Finest Hour" speech and we wouldn't
have cared. Our pride was hurt. Not injured, but hurt. In order to
fix it, we needed to earn some respect in the second half. We had
overcome larger deficits with less time, our goal was reachable.

By the time the Blue Hose kicked off to us, we had snapped
out of our mopey mood and were ready to play the last half of
the game with passion. Ready to snap the 12-game losing streak
to the Blue Hose. Ready to start our own winning streak! Helmets
nodded up and down to the tune of the band and teammates
chattered encouraging words as we lined up to return the kickoff.

The ball soared through the air and I locked eyes on the defender I was assigned to block, the fourth man in from the right. He
didn't see me coming for the right ear hole in his helmet. His eyes
were locked on Tavares darting back near the 15. He slowed down,
he might be ready to make a cut. His blue jersey and white helmet

Defensive lineman Phil Jordan (92), linebacker Anthony Moore (8),
and the rest of the defense struggled to get off PC blocks the entire game.

might as well have been a big red bulls-eye.

I squared my shoulders perpendicular to his so I didn't pick up a penalty. He still didn't see me. This is for the first touchdown.

CRACK

My facemask grazed his chin and his arms shot up in surprise. He stumbled off his path. Good, stick with him. Keep him out of his lane. Hands...

BEEEP

Tavares brought the ball out to the 29-yard line. Enthusiastically, we sprinted off the field with renewed hope for the game.

"Put some points on the board!" I shouted at Collin over my mouthpiece.

The offense prepared to march 71 yards and put us back in the game. Mills had thought of the right plays to call and Collin, along with the rest of the offensive unit, was ready to execute them.

Until Dre was stopped two yards behind the line of scrimmage on the first play.

"Get it back right here!"

No matter, next play. Sacked for a loss of five.

"Come on fellas, let's convert here!"

Sacked, again. Collin had fumbled and somebody wearing a blue jersey sprinted past the defensive bench toward the locker rooms. Touchdown Blue Hose. 28-0 within 2:00 of the second half starting.

We started the game with over 1,400 fans in the stands. After that last touchdown numbers dropped to about 200 friends and family who had no choice but to stay.

We never recovered. Offense never penetrated their 20-yard

line to even try and score. We held the ball for over 34 minutes, but we turned it over three times and we ended nine drives with punts. We played undisciplined, accumulating 10 penalties for 59 yards. We let The Blue Hose run up 374 yards of total offense on us. They rammed the football down our throats and then proceeded to dominate us in all three phases of the game. Offensively we were shut down by an interception, four sacks, and a forced fumble returned for a touchdown. We missed two field goals while we were still attempting them during the first two quarters of the game.

We embarrassed ourselves on offense, defense, and special teams. We didn't lose this game, Presbyterian College beat us. And they beat us by 42 points. I looked up at the fancy new scoreboard as we were herded off the field by an enraged coaching staff.

"CSU - 0."

– – –

Coach Mills didn't use curse words, that wasn't generally accepted at a Christian university. He didn't need any after that performance.

"Men, I don't know what else to say about this game so I'm going to leave it at that," he said. At first, I thought he was angry, an emotion I was familiar with. But that wasn't it. "I have one final announcement to make" his silver hair was soaked with sweat and I finally pinned down hurt worse than any curse words ever could.

Coach Mills met every one of us with his stare. Maybe he would say something about Sunday treatments for the hurt and injured among us. Maybe he would say something about our scheduled lift and meetings on Monday. I don't care, just get me out of this pitiful locker room so I could hide out in my dorm for the rest of the weekend.

"We'll have practice on Monday afternoon. Treatments tomorrow like normal. No lift or meeting on Monday. The next time we'll be together is Monday afternoon. In full pads."

To view more images from the PC game, go to http://BelieveEG21.com/presbyterian

CHAPTER 20

FULL PADS

MONDAY, SEPTEMBER 12, 2005

NORTH CHARLESTON, SC

We found plenty of time to think during the next 36 hours. Teammates conversed about pride and humility and why we lost. Why was it so bad? 42-0 was sad. It wasn't a game plan that fell through, it was our attitude. We erroneously thought we were a "good enough" team to show up and beat somebody. Somebody we'd never beat before in the history of the program. Somebody who taught us a lesson about ego that still stung today.

"Most of the time I get excited to be in this stinky locker room," I told Okeba as we gradually changed into our pads, "but today just feels weird."

"I know, it doesn't feel right," he said without looking at me. He sat across from me in his girdle, just holding his pads with his belt half-way inserted into his pants. He needed a haircut. He was staring at some far off place, far from this musky carpet. "I have a bad feeling about today."

"Yep, somebody's definitely getting hurt today," Mish, the

eternal cynic, chimed in from a few lockers down.

"Don't say that! Everything's gonna be fine." I attempted to convince them, and myself, of my words. "We're gonna have a tough practice, we'll beat each other up for a bit, and we'll all feel better. Then we'll go eat some bad food from the Caf and call it a night."

David and Okeba started taking bets while they riled up the rest of our half of the locker room. I didn't want any part of the conversation. I needed to get my mind right for this practice.

We dressed in full pads for a reason, though none of us really knew what that reason was yet. As soon as we finished stretching we plunged into full scrimmage mode.

"Going LIVE!" hollered Coach Kelly. Thrill crept from the corners of his mouth. This was the old school type of football the old offensive line coach loved.

We, on the other hand, were not enjoying practice as much as him. The scrimmage started slow. Like sparring partners who are unsure of the other's intentions or intensity, none of us wanted to throw the inevitable first punch. Our pride and our bodies were still bruised from the game 48 hours prior.

Live scrimmages consisted of the starting offense going against the starting defense at full speed. We would throw everything we had at each other like rams head-butting until one falls over from exhaustion. Then the second offense would go against the second defense. Repeating until tenderized. Cutting below the waist was live and whistles were not blown early. Tackles did not count simply by "tagging off," like most practices during the season. With the exception of quarterbacks, ball carriers were taken all the way to the ground. Just like a game.

The pity that accompanied us onto the field slowly burned off. We realized that last year's team would have accepted this loss and moved on. But we couldn't. We wouldn't. We came to realize, that all this "punishment" was what we needed. If the coaches let us accept that kind of loss, they wouldn't be doing their job. Theirs was to motivate us. Ours was to compete. And since we didn't do that Saturday, now was the time to do it.

The atmosphere sped up. The offensive and defensive lines sprinted to line up on the ball. The defensive backfield yapped at the offense in between coverages. Hits were heavy and pads popped powerfully. Backs opted for contact instead of taking a step out of bounds. Practice had transformed into a battlefield.

Bubble screen to Price: 15-yard gain. Coach Barrows and Perkins made offhand comments about why we didn't play like this Saturday. Sack by Degraf: seven-yard loss. We high fived, careful not to celebrate too much. Scramble by Collin: three-yard gain. More trash talk. Tough inside run by Robert: four-yard gain.

"Two's!" said Coach Chadwell as he threw up a peace sign.

Our break was short. This wasn't supposed to be punishment, but it sure felt like it. We lined up for another round of ones versus ones and my legs felt heavy. I could only imagine what the guys who played more than me felt like. The sweat pouring out of me mixed with the dirt from the torn upfield converted to a film of mud covering me from helmet to cleats. Kenny Harper, one of our tailbacks, caught a swing pass to the offensive right, out the flats. I was up. I sprinted to meet him in between the numbers and the sideline, forcing him back into my help in the middle of the field. He lowered his shoulder as I rushed in for contact. I was the first man on the scene so I stood him up and forced him toward the rest of the pursuit. My hands were up high on his body since he was a little meatball of a man when Jada Ross came flying in to finish him off. Jada smashed into us both for an ear-ringing assist and all three of us toppled to the ground.

Kenny got up and patted us both on the heads. "Good hit fellas!" he said as he tossed the football to Chadwell and ran to the huddle for the next call.

I wanted to tell him the same, but my attention was drawn

elsewhere. When I got up my thumb throbbed and my teeth clenched into my molded mouthpiece. No time to get off the field, only third down. I took a deep breath, and caught the signal from Coach Barrows: "Garnet." My right hand was fairly useless when Bryan Meers got his long arms on me and drove me off the ball. Fortunately, the ball was run to the opposite side for the next two plays and I could protect my hand from contact.

"Good job, One D!" yelled Coach Barrows. He leaned forward and applauded us as we exited the field, giving low fives where he could. I snuck to his right and stuck out my left hand, protecting my right as much as possible.

I ran to Andy, an athletic trainer on the sideline, and told him I needed to have my thumb wrapped before I went back in.

"Dude! What did you do?" were his first words. Awesome. His eyes grew large and his blonde eyebrows perked up as his eyes floated from my right thumb to my eyes and back down again.

I explained what happened and that I was fine, it just needed to be taped. I had to go back in, practice wasn't over. I didn't have time to waste, the first defense was almost up and I had a starting job to protect. Andy begrudgingly agreed on the premise that I would come back to see him as soon as practice ended. Without taking my hand out of my glove, he taped it as tight as he could to keep it from swelling any more.

Andy, Toby and the rest of the athletic training staff had a hard job. Their responsibilities were to protect us and heal us while not letting us get away with cheating the team. Toby was always asking, "Are you hurt or are you injured?" Although the question popped into my mind, I didn't give myself enough time to think about the answer.

"First and 10!" said Coach Kelly. "Let's go, Ones! Wiggle! No walking!" My cue.

The rest of practice went smooth. As smooth as a violent game like football can be, at least. We played well on defense and the offense clicked with each other. We carried the intensity through to the end. By sundown, none of us were complaining about being in full pads. The brutality had somehow strained away some of our collective ego. As we knelt down for announcements, praises, and prayer requests Coach Mills could tell we had been humbled.

"Men, this could have been par for the course if we let it." Coach Mills spoke calmly. The look of embarrassment had been replaced with pride. "Which is why we practiced today. This is a new team. In a new era. And we have so much to prove. We weren't out to accept mediocrity, much less be blown out by a team that wasn't in our division of play." He wasn't reading from his notes, he was speaking from the heart without a script. "This practice wasn't about getting something off my chest. This is about the team knowing how poorly we played and that we have enough pride to not let you accept that defeat. Today was a consequence for Saturday. We had to pay for that poor performance by going full pads today. Practice became spirited, we came alive today!" His fists were clenched and his chest puffed out behind his gray coaching t-shirt, he was proud of how we competed. "This. This practice. This intensity. This is what we want every Saturday. And these are the kinds of practices we need, as well, too. This is what it will take for us to win that conference championship we've all been talking about."

We hated it, but he was right. We fought harder today, in front of nobody, than we had on Saturday at our first home game of the year.

When announcements were wrapped up I crept into the Athletic Training Center to see Andy about my bulging thumb. "Why do you still have your glove on?" he asked when I sat down on the navy blue training table. "And why is it soaking wet? You know this is a medical facility, Mike. We can't have you dripping wet...."

"It won't come off," I cut him off with a sheepish look before he could finish his rant. "It's swollen so big I can't get my glove off my hand. And it's soaking wet because I had to shower with it on. I'm clean. Can you cut it off, please?"

Andy held back a laugh and took out his scissors to cut me free. Before he could get an ice bag filled, my hand swelled to look like a golf ball was cut in two with one half placed on the top of my hand and the other half stuck to my palm.

Soon Toby was brought over to discuss what happened and diagnose the problem. He usually had something to make me laugh or an insult to fling my way. Not today.

"Mike, I hate to tell you this," Toby said, sounding as if he was about to pull off a band-aid. "But, I think it's broken."

CHAPTER 21

CONVOCATION

WEDNESDAY, SEPTEMBER 14, 2005

NORTH CHARLESTON, SC

"Hey! Over here," with my left hand I waved at CJ and pointed to an open seat next to mine. I saw him raise a pointed finger and walk down the sloped maroon carpet toward me through the crowd of students. I plopped down into the blue knotted padding of the folding chair and exhaled in harmony with the squeaking of the seat. I watched bodies aimlessly buzzing in the seats ahead of me, waiting for the opening ceremonies. The worn auditorium seats felt much more comfortable than the classroom chairs I'd just spent an hour fidgeting in.

My low back was sore and my legs were tight from Monday's practice. I was used to getting much more rest than this and my body was letting me know it. I could deal with all the minor ailments, but the throbbing in my thumb was new. I had been put in a sling to keep the blood from rushing into my thumb and causing more pain. The swelling had gone down according to the doctors, but not enough for me to notice. The X-rays they showed me just 24-hours before revealed a shattered thumb, broken into three pieces.

"Hey dude, thanks," said CJ as he sank down into the chair next to mine and began taking off his backpack. "How does your thumb feel?"

"Eh. It's still attached," I said with as much humor as I could muster. "I just want to get this surgery done as soon as possible so they can tell me if I'll be able to play or not at the end of the season."

"When is it?"

"After we play JU," I said. "I'll have to miss the North Greenville game because the surgery is on a Thursday and I'll need a day or two to recover. Mom is coming up for it."

The lights dimmed and we put our conversation on pause for the presentation. The Chapel, the same one in which we held Eddie's final ceremony, was used for a number of gatherings, including Convocation. Every other Wednesday "Convo," as we called it, was held for the school. Attendance was mandatory, though it didn't always translate to paying attention; all under-graduates were required to attend a certain number to graduate. Convo was also mandatory for staff, including coaches. Coaches Chadwell and Perkins, being sleep-deprived as they were, took the opportunity to nap in the empty upper balcony. CJ and I, like the coaches, found a loophole in the system. If we took night classes, we wouldn't technically be considered full-time students. If we weren't considered full-time students, we needed to attend less Convo's to graduate. We took full advantage. This was the only convo we'd have to attend all year so we didn't mind sitting through it.

Sometimes a speaker would address the school and other times a group would perform. Today, we had a guest speaker who was being introduced by Dr. Jairy Hunter, the president of the university. His invocations were typically funny, although we weren't exactly itching to be entertained. We were still feeling the hangover from PC. The embarrassment of our loss became more intense as we spent more time with regular students.

Dr. Hunter cracked some jokes as he tried to get everyone to loosen up and begin to pay attention while he went into happenings around campus. "How many of y'all are ready for the new science building?" he polled as he scanned the upper and lower decks. "It's a beautiful building and we'll have classes beginning next semester." A mandatory round of applause half-way filled the room before he continued. "If you got a chance to go to the football game this weekend, you probably saw our new scoreboard. It's too bad we couldn't put any points on it."

Before he could go on, the entire auditorium exploded with laughter and a wave of "oooooooooh" was directed at football players across the auditorium. CJ and I looked at each other with a did-he-just-say-that look. As the murmurs began we spotted other players around us that had popped their heads up like gophers in search of other players and coaches. When we would lock eyes we shook our heads in disbelief that our own president had mocked us so openly.

We thought we had relieved the stigma of "The Bad News Bears of College Football" a year earlier with our 5-5 season. We figured there would be a supportive air about the campus and everyone would give us the respect we "deserved." Dr. Hunter's statement made it apparent that everyone, except us, had already forgotten last season. But nobody cared what happened last year. Nobody cared who we could be or what we did in the past. A Coach Perkins saying popped into my head, "Potential is nothing, performance is everything."

The last bit of confidence we had built up came crashing down. We hadn't performed and we were faced with an embarrassing reality. We started our "dream season" 0-2 and we were coming off of one of the worst losses in school history. We sank below the high wooden arms of the folding seats and fumed as Convo seemed to drag on for an eternity.

An hour later, after dismissal, CJ and I huddled with other teammates asking, "What was that all about?" and "Why would he say that?" Most of us were downright angry. We had fought so hard to try and rid ourselves of the stigma of a losing team. We thought we were past these embarrassing cracks after the first non-losing season in team history the year prior.

We were upset. Not because we had been called out, but because on some level we knew Dr. Hunter was right. We were talking trash and we were steaming, but we needed that to happen. Our rose-colored glasses had been shattered and we knew we had work to do. This was our wake-up call. Almost winning was nothing to brag about. Coming close to winning wasn't what we wanted. It took this sort of embarrassment from our own supporters to bring that truth to the surface. Many times a university will back it's team during highs and lows, but we had not earned the respect of our fans.

Those of us that came from successful high school and junior college programs knew what it was like to be part of a winning program. Non-losing and winning are two different mentalities. We were halfway kidding ourselves, but we wanted that mentality to shift just because we had stepped on campus. "Things are different now," was something I heard dozens of times over the past 12 months. In reality, we hadn't done enough to be considered a winning team. Namely, winning.

At 0-2, undefeated was out of the question. Our dreams of a championship were far from shattered, but one thing was certain, we had work to do.

CHAPTER 22

JACKSONVILLE UNIVERSITY

SATURDAY, SEPTEMBER 17, 2005

NORTH CHARLESTON, SC

Jacksonville University was technically a Division 1-AA program, the same as Charleston Southern. With one slight difference; they could not offer athletic scholarships. This gave us, in theory, a major advantage over the Dolphins because we now had a full roster of scholarships thanks to Coach Mills' creative accounting. However, we still felt the aftermath of the Presbyterian loss, something Mills hoped to shake after Monday's full padded practice.

From the sideline I watched JU's first kickoff go soaring through the back of our endzone: touchback. The sun pounded our skin, the air was stagnant, and the stands were empty – typical home game. My jersey, like everyone else's was soaked with perspiration. Unlike them, I wasn't in full gear. I was dressed in a sweat-stained Bucs hat, my stinky cast, and some khaki shorts that my jersey was tucked into. I pushed my way to the sideline to get a better view of what was happening on the field. I pressed against sweaty bodies and bulky shoulder pads, feeling like I'd somehow shrunk without my pads. I could hear sweat pouring from their skin and I couldn't possibly be more jealous.

To sit on the sidelines and watch, helplessly, as someone took my spot on the kickoff team was painful. But, that pain was nothing compared to hearing "Starting defense!" and taking a step toward the sideline, only to realize that no longer included me. I was resigned to being the go-between from Coach Perkins in the sky box and the DB's on the sideline. I had become an unofficial member of the coaching staff with my sweaty hat and two-way handheld radio.

On the field, the offense had already fumbled on their third play. Not the start we wanted. After we swapped fumbles and the offense failed to convert a fourth and three, JU took over and started to put drives together. I was frustrated as I had to watch from the sideline while someone else played "my" position. Okeba Rollinson came into the program with me the year prior. He was extremely intelligent, although he didn't want everyone to know it. He was the kind of player who was described by all, including himself, as "lazy, but talented." He came to camp without having touched a weight or attempting a sprint, yet managed to find himself on the field starting the first game of the season in place of Tavares who was serving his punishment for showing up late to camp.

Okeba had pinned me as a leader the year prior when I offered to host a study session of the playbook during our first preseason camp. "I'm just gonna follow Mike and CJ," regularly came from him and David Misher. He knew he was as good, if not better, than me. He never thought he'd have the chance to reveal his skill, knowing it would be hard to beat out a starter who knew every scheme inside out, worked hard at every turn, and who played like a coach on the field. Like a phony, he felt he had somehow snuck his way into a starting position without merit.

Before the game, he felt nervous and made me go over every situation imaginable with him. We sat side by side in the lockers as he asked me routine questions that I knew he knew the answer to. Normally he and Darius Jackson would cheat off of my pre-game test and be done with it. Not worrying about the potential consequences of being thrown into the game unexpectedly. Today was different. Today he kept his test and compared it to mine after Coach Perkins had already gone over the schemes. He was actually interested in knowing what to do in each situation. Eventually, his interest paid off.

Jacksonville came into the second quarter with mounting momentum. The Dolphins put the first points of the day on the board with a short field goal. As soon as this happened, a few shoulders slumped ever so slightly on the Buccaneer sideline. Some of the older, more experienced guys noticed this and weren't having any of it. Tempers flared from normally quieter defensive guys like Adam Degraffenreid and Tavares Shorter. They were leaders, but not the kind who would get in people's faces. Today, something shifted.

"Every Man, Every Play, Every Day!" they shouted, referencing the white banner we had tapped on the way out to the field. The white banner with our theme, our cutlass, and the commemoratory "EG21" black dot emblazoned on it. The banner that we had all signed as a sign of our dedication to each other. Their message was about accountability and how we owed it to each other to play our best at all times. The message had Eddie Gadson's work ethic all over it.

Before we could fall into a hole, backs straightened and chinstraps buckled. We stopped feeling sorry for ourselves and got back to work.

With 4:03 left in the second quarter, the Dolphins tried to pick on Okeba. The right tackle crashed down into our weak side linebacker, Jada Ross, and the beginning of a "zone read" play formed on the offense's right side. The tight end who was lined up across from Okeba lurched toward him, trying to push him toward the sideline. Okeba recognized this and gave up a little ground. I got nervous, he should attack the tight end and shrink the lane that's beginning to form. The quarterback had taken the snap and had his hands low and to his left, feeling for the tailback's belly. The whole time his eyes were on the gap where Okeba and Jada needed to be. Okeba was giving ground and Jada seemed to be pinned inside with a guard pulling to clean up anybody in the way. All of the sudden Jada threw the tackle to the ground and took on the pulling guard, stuffing the open hole.

I watched impatiently from the sideline as the play developed, calling out everything as it happened. "Run! Run! Run! It's comin' your way Keeb! Comin' left! Left!"

A white jersey with a green number 26 popped out from the would-be hole in the offensive line to make a dash at the sideline. He saw his tight end in front of Okeba and gained ground, heading to the first down marker four short yards away. Okeba recognized the outside move just in time and avoided the tight end's grasp by dipping his shoulder and aiming low on the tailback's thighs. As Okeba dove at his legs, the running back stuck out his left arm, ready to stiff-arm Okeba's helmet into the dirt and keep sprinting up the sideline.

Fortunately for us, the extra 30 pounds Okeba put on during his redshirt year helped him fly right through the back's legs. Okeba flipped him onto his outstretched arm with one single motion. He made a clean, open field tackle and popped up to check the first down marker.

"Fourth and one," signaled the sideline judge in front of us.

"Good job Keeb! Get out there, punt return team! Good job fellas, way to get off the field," I was proud of him and the rest of the defense. I began patting helmets, shoulder pads, and butts as they filed off the field. "Good job, bro!" I said as Okeba jog-walked straight at me behind our sideline. I believed in him, although I was not sure he believed in himself yet.

His small afro had indentations caused by the air pockets in his helmet and he was glistening with sweat. He was out of shape and out of breath, but he was excited. Before he could talk, he gave me five with his large, gloved hand and took a spot on the defensive bench. "Preciate it," was all he could muster. I grabbed him a water cup from the end of the bench and rubbed his sweaty afro, launching sweat beads everywhere in a two-foot radius. As I walked away to hand CJ the two-way radio, he hollered out, "I'm glad we went over those plays!"

His words were bitter-sweet to me and I gave him a half smile. Although he was playing well, I struggled to be happy for him. Selfishly, I wanted it to be me making that tackle.

The Dolphins held the lead until halftime. Collin and the offense had been driving all day, but couldn't seem to put any points on the board. Finally he connected with Drew Rucks, the transfer wide receiver from Purdue, for a 13-yard touchdown pass. We ended the second quarter with a 7-3 lead, hardly a dominating performance.

At the half we received an earful from Coach Mills. "They didn't come here to get beat! They came here to prove they don't need scholarships to play at our level! They didn't get the letter in the mail that we were supposed to win." Like a parent who knows what cuts their child deepest, he knew exactly how to get inside our heads.

We were emotionally drained, and the heat wasn't helping. We were a much better team than they were, but we weren't playing like it.

We came out in the third quarter and picked up where we left off. The offense couldn't put full drives together, but we continued to give them more chances on defense. Either we played good on offense or played good on defense, but we could never compile a complete game. One side of the ball would carry the other, limping through games until a fourth quarter showdown.

After we forced the fourth fumble of the day, Collin connected with Bryan Meers from one yard out to put us up by 10. I loved to see Bryan catching touchdown passes or doing well in a game.

Offensive linemen Troy James (74) and
Alex Bragg (64) listen intently for the play call.

His legendary catch against VMI the year prior was huge, but rare. He played more of a blocking tight end than a pass receiving one. As teammates you have competitions within the game and I had one with Bryan. He was an excellent blocker and got the best of me on multiple occasions. Except for the time I delivered him a concussion during camp. I called it even after that. For now, I was happy we were winning and that he got the chance for a catch and a touchdown.

The Dolphins came within six points with 9:09 left in the fourth quarter. Good defense, lead by Okeba's first collegiate interception, helped us keep it that way. We held JU off for the remainder of the game for a final score of 16-10. Although we picked up a win, it hardly felt like it.

Sometimes you crush teams you're "supposed to beat," and other times they show you your weaknesses. We had been exposed in more than a few areas. We still couldn't move the ball on the ground, netting only 26 rushing yards on 32 attempts. Our offense was becoming more consistent through the air, but we missed Eddie's hands as much as his leadership. On defense we continued to make big plays, but we gave up enough to let them hang with us until the fourth quarter. We beat JU because of raw talent but we still lacked maturity and the ability to play our game under any circumstances. Though you'd never be able to tell we won the game, we walked off the field relieved to earn our first win.

To view more images from the JU game, go to http://BelieveEG21.com/jacksonville

CHAPTER 23

NORTH GREENVILLE UNIVERSITY

SATURDAY, SEPTEMBER 24, 2005

NORTH CHARLESTON, SC/TIGERVILLE, SC

White linens extended for miles and pillows piled up around me like castle walls. The queen size mattress of the Fairfield Inn & Suites down the street was significantly more comfortable than my twin back in the Quads. I rarely had trouble falling asleep back in my dorm, but this bed was heaven. I weaved in and out of dreams as easily as the footwork drills Coach Perkins put us through in practice. The hum of College Gameday on ESPN from the flat screen TV provided just enough white noise to drown out Mom's business calls from the other side of the hotel room. Under the black plaster of a new cast my thumb throbbed from the structural addition of a metal plate and six screws.

This marked the second day of rehabilitation. The first day, mostly spent in the same bed surrounded by painkillers and textbooks, proved miserable after the surgery. The last thing I remembered clearly was Coach Perkins praying with me and Mom. She cherished his presence and his prayers.

I had previously come back from knee and ankle injuries but none that required surgery. Nothing like this. The last 12 months of my life had been spent preparing for this football season. The physical training enabled me to cope with the pain of the injury, but the mental misery of knowing that I wouldn't play again this year sickened me. My main focus in life was no longer in my control. I numbly gazed at the TV screen while these thoughts jumbled around in my brain. I could keep busy by helping the team and the athletic trainers said I could still workout. Plus, there was always school, but that's not why I came here. Football was over for the next year and there was nothing I could do about it. My first chance as a starter was gone.

At least Mom was here to keep me company. She was a good listener. In between drug-induced naps all I wanted to talk about was football. Why this shouldn't have happened to me, or anyone for that matter. How it would be hard to get back to where I was physically. I tried to be as stoic as I had been on the phone when I told her it was broke. But I couldn't hold it in and I knew she'd never judge me for expressing my disappointment.

The team had already left for The Upstate to face our next opponent, the North Greenville Crusaders. Though Division 2, they had just as many weapons as Presbyterian and posed a similar threat. The win against JU felt like a weight lifted off our shoulders, but we were still 1-2, not the record we expected. Undefeated was out of the question, but winning a conference championship was plausible; we didn't start conference play for another three games. This was our year. A win against NGU wouldn't mean much in the grand scheme, but it could be the confidence booster we needed.

Anticipation hung in the air all week at practice, like we wanted to hurry up and get past the Crusaders so we didn't mess it up. We knew the potential to be a better team was with us, but we had to show up. As Coach Perk regularly reminded us, "Potential is nothing, performance is everything."

As the day wore on, I insisted we listen to the radio broadcast of the game. Jon Davis, the campus pastor and ex-offensive line coach, called the game with the same intensity he brought to the pulpit on Sunday mornings. Through Jon's play-by-play analysis, I felt like I was on the field.

We started the game with a commanding series to set the tone, driving the ball 80 yards on eight plays. Robert "Bobby" Adams carried the workload from the running back position, racking up 21 yards on four carries. Bobby, who looked like a cross between the movie characters Forest Gump and Bobby Boucher from The Waterboy, was tall for a running back, standing 6'1". He ran straight up and down and sported a number 44 jersey, hence the Forest Gump references. This style should have given him a major disadvantage when it came time for contact from would-be tacklers, but that wasn't the case at all. Bobby avoided no one; he loved contact.

We commanded the game for the first three quarters without trailing. But with 13:16 left in the fourth quarter, NGU took the lead by a touchdown to go up 28-21. But this was different than any time we trailed before. Something was different about the way Jon called the plays. His voice translated a cool, calm attitude. We didn't panic. We played with composure, as if we knew we were going to win. We'd never been able to do this in the past. Though we were expected to beat this team, this was a big step for us.

After a battle of field position, Collin connected on a 53-yard pass all the way to the endzone. The longest reception of the day came at a pivotal moment. We tied the game 28-28 with 7:58 left on the clock.

North Greenville put a drive together quickly, picking up a tough third down and 13 yards. But David Misher had other plans. David, a walk-on the year prior, played without being on full scholarship. He had bounced around from receiver to cornerback in 2004 because he was smart, had fast feet, and could catch. He earned a blue jersey during 5:30 a.m. workouts and played savvy football, always spotting seemingly small tendencies others overlooked. He intercepted a pass at the NGU 40-yard line and returned it 22 yards to give us possession, a short field, and most importantly, the momentum we needed to close out the game.

Bobby eventually scored from two yards out to seal the game. He wasn't the regular starter that game, but he stepped up for us. His tough running style proved helpful against NGU, amassing 124 rushing yards and another 31 receiving out of the backfield. Players that hadn't started the season were making an impact on offense and defense; a strong sign of a winning team. Bobby stepped in for Dre, the regular starter. Okeba stepped in the week prior at JU to fill my spot. And Markus Murry, the freshman receiver from Chicago, stepped in to fill Eddie's spot in his own way.

Markus totaled 61 yards on four catches with a long reception of 21 yards coming in the fourth quarter on a crucial third-down and 18. Markus didn't know Eddie except for his recruiting trip when Eddie drove him an hour and a half in his gold Saturn to Columbia, South Carolina just to show his recruit a fun time. That selflessness, a trademark quality of Eddie's, was enough to know how strong of a teammate Eddie would have been. If the other guys on the team were half as committed, he knew he'd feel at home for the next four years. Eddie was part of the reason Markus still honored his commitment to CSU after Michigan State University offered him a scholarship earlier that summer. Eddie would have been proud of Markus' performance at North Greenville.

Over the airwaves and through Jon Davis' voice, I could sense that something had matured in us. We found a way to win, a feat elusive to us since our big victory over VMI. The best teams aren't the ones with the best individual players, they're the ones who play the best as a whole. We didn't beat North Greenville because of one or two or even three players. We won because we were able to pull together as a team, something we'd have to get used to doing if we wanted to keep winning.

Back in the hotel room, I loved the rare quiet time with Mom, she kept me positive while I moped. Although the circumstances were not ideal, I think I gave her as much of a lift as she did me. I

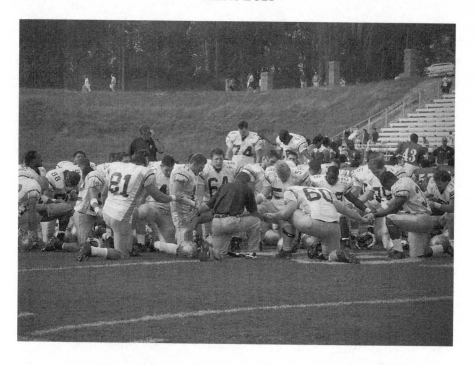

No matter the outcome, we "locked it up" to recite The Lord's Prayer after each game. On this day we were thankful for a win.

appreciated her coming to spend time with me, but I was happy to be back in the company of my teammates in the Quads the next morning. At this stage in my life, their support rivaled Mom's.

     I congratulated the guys and asked how they played individually. It seemed as though they had been dealt a hand of humility since I saw them last. Nobody boasted on themselves, only on others. I heard about Bobby and David and Markus' plays from every angle. I was proud of the individuals and I made sure to tell them so. We needed some sense of self if we were going to beat Howard the next week.

To view more images from the North Greenville game, go to http://BelieveEG21.com/ngu

CHAPTER 24

HOWARD UNIVERSITY

SATURDAY, OCTOBER 1, 2005

NORTH CHARLESTON, SC

Somewhere between the North Greenville victory and this morning's pre-game meal, we regained confidence. The first four
games of the season humbled us and we weren't nearly as high on
ourselves as we were during camp. We stabilized for the first time
since opening day. With a win today, we could head into conference play with a winning record, something unheard of for CSU.

Our conversations were stuffed full of anticipation about the
upcoming game. We discussed game plans and potential pitfalls,
pointing out their weaknesses as well as our own. We studied
Howard's quarterback and his arsenal of weapons. Collin and the
offense watched film of their safety, Antione Bethea, erasing ground
faster than the delete button on a keyboard. NFL material, for sure.
The coaches preached that they were no different than us, but the
Bison would be a tough team to beat.

Many conversations didn't take place. We didn't talk about
how we missed our opportunity to beat them the year prior. We

didn't talk about how we were distracted, possibly intimidated, by the historically black university's atmosphere as much as their team. We didn't talk about how we blew it with a botched fake punt or the infamous fake field goal, "Tora Tora Tora" in the last half of the game. Plays that would have been genius calls, except for that safety, Bethea.

This year, things were different. They were coming to our field where the atmosphere was comfortable and there were no drum lines or dance squads to distract us from the task at hand. We approached this game differently, like somehow it mattered more. Reality set in: if our play doesn't change, we might be average. Again. We worked hard during camp and all season, but this week we pushed just a little more. Practices were sharp and meetings were focused. Position groups held player-led film sessions in the Quads up until the night before kickoff. This year was different.

Buccaneer Stadium typically provided two distinct home field advantages: the noise and the heat. 1,200 fans can only be so intimi-

Linebacker Jada Ross (54) and a gang of defensive linemen prepare to stop a third-down and short against the Howard Bison.

dating, no matter how avid they may be. In reality, the entire audience could squeeze into the middle section of the stadium beneath "BUCCANEERS" with room to spare. To us, the quiet atmosphere was just another home game. To the Bison, and other visiting teams, our home crowds were as exciting as a scrimmage. The deafening heat, stuck on maximum for another few weeks, was muffled by a rare breeze that helped practice kicks sail a few additional yards North toward the field house.

Today, the atmosphere was familiar. The small crowd and the warm breeze gave us a minute advantage, something we quickly exploited. Tavares, who had been playing like an all-conference safety since being benched for the first game, intercepted Howard's quarterback in the first series and returned it down to their 12-yard line. Less than a minute into the game our offense drove through their red zone, the supplementary film was already paying off. Drew Rucks caught a quick pass from Collin and Kenny Harper found the endzone two yards later: 7-0.

The remainder of the first quarter went according to plan. Despite the wind, Nick Ellis kicked a field goal and we pushed the Bison back for a safety all within the first 12 minutes of the game. Confidence swelled and the shiny blue scoreboard read 12-0 at the end of the first quarter.

The Bison, a mature team, were not shaken by our quick start. They were busy assembling an impressive drive with large chunks of yardage. 13 yards to start the drive, 10 more to back it up, five more, 10 more after that. The drive, which we called a "fluke," ended with a touchdown.

Nick answered with an immediate field goal after a sloppy drive filled with incomplete passes, sacks and penalties. The precision with which we started the game faded on both sides of the ball. Routes were rounded and tackling attempts became sloppy.

Suddenly, chunks of field started to disappear. At half, Howard led 21-15 after they compiled two more "fluke" drives ending in touchdowns.

During halftime the coaches made adjustments to schemes and we shared what we saw on the field. Their quarterback, Ronald Venters, completing 11 for 12 passes on the last few drives was unacceptable. Coach Barrows made it clear the secondary had to tighten up coverage. Tavares, who was all over the field, sucked his teeth and shook his head. Coach Perkins defended the DB's by adding that we needed more pressure from the defensive line and some help in coverage from our linebackers. After all, we couldn't cover for 10 seconds each time Venters dropped back to pass.

Over top the wooden lockers, Coach Kelly smoldered over the offensive line's lack of push up front. Without a ground game, Collin became an easy target for stunting defensive linemen. Coach Mills warned Collin to keep the ball out of Bethea's reach, he was everywhere. If we found ourselves in a Two-Minute Drill, with the pressure to score quick, he could be the game changer.

Roles reversed and we started the second half as slow as Howard had begun the first, drudging only 15 yards in six plays before being forced to punt. The Bison started their drive with vengeance, gambling on a trick play aimed at stunning and confusing us if executed properly. Their first play, an end around executed with perfection, left our defensive linemen chasing the wrong man and the defensive backs turning on their heels for an impossible pursuit angle. 65 yards later, we sat stunned and confused, down 27-15.

The misdirection play, which had never appeared on film, left the defense bickering on the sideline while the offense started a volley of field position that would spill into the fourth quarter. The Bison, setting up for a 37-yard field goal attempt, had just pieced together a 17-play drive when we caught our second wind. We had stiffened up on defense to stop them from putting in a touchdown, but a field goal would still put them two touchdowns and a two-point conversion ahead of us.

Phil Jordan, our Samoan defensive lineman who had been recruited from a California JUCO, put his big hand in the ground between the long snapper and the left guard. The ball spiraled back

Coach Kelly (headset), explaining why jumping offside
is a bad thing or potentially ripping someone for not
doing their job, did not have patience for mental mistakes.

to the holder and Phil pierced the wall of linemen just far enough
to get his taped paw in the ball's projected path. The thud of the
block sent a wave of cheers through the sideline that was not only
relieving, but invigorating.

Before Phil could finish pounding his chest and stomping out
his lack of intimidation toward the Howard sideline, the offense had
already huddled around Mills for our next opportunity. The game
was close and we needed two scores to retake the lead we lost back
in the second quarter. Our running game struggled against the
Bison front and passing plays would save valuable time. Mills, without hesitation, decided the ball needed to be in the air this series.

Collin could only complete three of four passes before Maurice
Price broke a hitch-and-go route for 65 yards, cutting Howard's
lead to five. The momentum had shifted and our enthusiasm built
with every second. The hard work was paying off, the visualization

exercises were working, we would have one more opportunity to win this game!

Howard started their next offensive series with a furious 30-yard pass to Williams, the player who carried the end around. Fortunately, Marvin was in good position at cornerback to bring him down around midfield and save a touchdown. Tavares and the defense pushed them back over midfield and forced a punt three plays later, burning only 1:55 on the clock

The offense adjusted for the abundance of time on the clock, 7:38 was way more than they needed. Mills would have to be strategic about play calls. If we scored too fast, they'd have time to come back on us. If we took too long and didn't score, they would burn the clock for the win.

We started smooth, shaving off 20 yards with the first two plays and eventually facing a manageable third down and three from our own 48-yard line. Collin dropped back but pass protection broke down before he could find an open receiver. Sacked: 12 yard loss. Coach Kelly stared a hole through the offensive line as they trotted to the sideline, not one daring to meet his look. That look that nobody could hide from.

Stranded deep in our own territory, we couldn't attempt fourth and 15, not with more than five minutes on the game clock. Mills was forced to assemble the punt team, hoping Howard would turn the ball back over to us.

Howard struck at the opportunity to close out the game. They meticulously ran the ball on five of the next six plays, chewing up the clock by standing up slow and using every available second of the game clock. Like a balloon being released of its air, our enthusiasm escaped with every yard the Bison gained. The final blow came with a 25-yard rush, giving the Bison their final first down of the day. They ran down the clock with ease, the final score dangling just in front of us, 27-22.

The additional practice could never teach us to keep our

emotions in check like was needed during the second half. The player-led film sessions taught us their plays, but we could never fully grasp how deep we would have to dig to retake the lead from a more seasoned team. We were tempted to say the extra reps didn't matter, but we knew that wasn't true. All the added work mattered, it just wasn't enough.

HAIL TO THEE O CHAR-LESTON SOUTH-ERN...

The horns of the band blared and we faced the blue scoreboard for the singing of the alma mater. Helmets were held by the facemasks, each pointing toward the afternoon sky. Eyes anchored firmly in the grass. Each game seemed to teach an excruciating lesson, one after the other.

HO-NOR, COU-RAGE, FAITH AND JUS-TICE...

Technically, this loss didn't affect our standings in the conference. But morale couldn't take too many more games like this. Individuals stepped up, but we had yet to finish a game against a formidable opponent.

AL-MA MA-TER HAIL

"C-S-U!"

We limped off the field at 2-3 with seven days to prepare for VMI, our first conference opponent.

To view more images from the Howard game, go to http://BelieveEG21.com/howard

CHAPTER 25

VIRGINIA MILITARY INSTITUTE

SATURDAY, OCTOBER 8, 2005

LEXINGTON, VA

"Touchdown Keydets!"

The strength and abruptness of the announcement were second only to the cannon blast that was sure to follow. VMI's "Wing-T" offense had gotten the best of us, again. Apparently, they were a bit salty about our win last year. Nobody wants to give a team their first conference victory in school history, especially not a group of prideful military school Keydets.

BANG

I had stopped jumping at the sound of the cannon, this was the fourth time we'd experienced it. The first shot rang 3:26 into the game. VMI marched 75 yards for a tone-setting score and hadn't taken prisoners since. They added two more touchdowns and a safety to give themselves a 22-0 lead halfway through the third quarter.

Maybe it was the eight-hour road trip to Lexington, Virginia that threw us off our game. Maybe it was the wild sea of white Keydet uniforms that forced us to drop four passes and fumble twice. Maybe it was the distracting mountain known as Alumni Memorial Field's home bleachers, packed with nearly 7,000 fans, that helped block the field goal on our first drive.

It couldn't be that we were too confident in ourselves. It couldn't be that we assumed this would be an easy win, "because we did it last year." Surely it couldn't be that a disciplined football team stuck to their game plan and wanted it more than us.

The Buccaneer team that suited up today was more talented and experienced than the 2004 team who beat them in the last 30 seconds of the game. We had more offensive weapons and a more seasoned defensive unit. We had something bigger than ourselves to play for!

But, we didn't have Eddie, who caught 10 passes and sparked the 21-point run leading to our victory with a touchdown grab. We didn't have the same leaders on the team who could pull us out of slumps like this. We didn't have the maturity to fight back from a deficit and tell guys to, "Keep your heads up, still a lot of football to be played!"

Collin and the offense, out of sheer embarrassment, muscled through an 11-play drive for our first score of the day with five minutes left in the third quarter. His position afforded him leadership status and he possessed all the physical gifts, but something was missing. Although we moved the ball 67 yards in five minutes, we still finished the drive sloppily. VMI blocked our extra point attempt.

A moment of déjà vu sparked when the ensuing kickoff was fumbled by the returner and recovered by Okeba, who was making more plays every week. 22-6 was a smaller deficit to overcome than last year and more time was left on the clock. Collin rush for two. Rucks completion for four. Adams rush for six. First down CSU. Adams again for three.

The string of four positive plays surprised the Keydets and the third quarter ended on a positive note for our sideline. The changing of quarters gave us the opportunity to inject a shot of hope into the situation. Positivity flowed like Gatorade from the spigots of our coolers. The defense came off the bench to support the huddling offense with pats on the helmet and words of encouragement. The game plan was simple: start executing assignments. All week, preparation consisted of reminders from the previous season: we outplayed them, we outlasted them, we finished. Do it again! The coaches had built up our confidence and this was the time to prove them right.

Mills and Collin discussed the remainder of the drive between water bottle squirts, throwing out potential plays and scenarios given the short field and race against the clock. The field was all but covered by the long shadow of the stadium as the offense hustled to their positions, ready to strike.

The hope was short-lived. Collin threw an interception just 20 yards shy of the goal line on the first play of the fourth quarter.

On the immediate drive, the Keydets proceeded down the field with the exact precision expected of a military parade. Two-yard dive up the middle. 12-yard toss sweep to the field. Six-yard counter to the weak side. Play after play they fell into formation, displaying neither complaint nor celebration. 17-yard play action pass complete, just to keep us on our toes. The parade came to close with an eight-yard option, kept by the quarterback, followed by a three-yard dive. The touchdown capped a 16-play drive and another shot thundered from the cannon.

BANG

We answered with a score, but it was too little and way too late. Their starters were already removing their pads and celebrating with the student section behind the bench while we "competed" against their third string. We fell to 2-4 on the year,

0-1 in the conference. VMI ran away with our first conference game of the season.

– – –

Underneath the face of concrete bleachers, water dripped from crevices in the low roof, splattering into unzipped travel bags that lie ready to be packed. "First, we will be the best. Then, we will be first." Mills post-game speech was hardly inspiring, even he had trouble believing his own words. "We will break it down how we see ourselves, as champions. Jada, get us out of here."

Never one for speeches, Jada forewent the words of encouragement he was entitled to give. "Champs on two, champs on two... One! Two!"

"Champs!" came out with mandatory enthusiasm. Emotion was hard to fake after the drain of a loss. Although I hadn't played, I was just as invested in the game as any of my teammates. Everything seemed to move slower after a loss. There wasn't just a lack of smiles, there was an abundance of frowns. Disappointment pervaded the team. We left the cramped locker room and loaded the buses for a miserably silent journey home.

– – –

Coach Mills, sitting solo at the head of the offensive bus, meticulously pored over his notes from pre-game. What went wrong? Why did we come so unraveled? Was the game plan wrong? Did he let the players get too cocky? Did they still believe a championship could be won? His mind raced with mathematical equations as he dug up the conference schedule. He scanned the calendar and, with a sigh of relief, leaned back in his seat. This was the first conference game of the season, he had three games and a bye week to prepare the team for Gardner Webb, the next conference opponent. The team with a nationally ranked offense. The first step in the gauntlet of games that comprised conference play. During the next month, the remainder of our opponents would round robin, finishing conference play with their game against us.

He took a break from his notes, he had seven and a half more hours to review them anyway. He tried to enjoy the first reds and yellows of fall foliage along Route 501 South, but the uncomfortably familiar colors reminded him of VMI's crisp uniforms. He needed a reviving sermon in the morning, something to refresh his heart and his spirit, something he could share with his team. His mind jumped from ideas about practice to methods for inspiring the team to the coming game against the Bobcats of West Virginia Wesleyan. Did the Bucs see themselves as he had forced them to break it down... as Champs?

– – –

"We're definitely the worst team in the conference." Okeba's whisper was uncomfortably loud at the opposite end of the defensive bus. Like an air horn going off in the library during finals week, his comments were impossible to miss. Jon Carmon, Mish, Okeba, and a rotating cast of participants engaged in ongoing arguments about everything. Today's topic was our ability to win out the rest of the season. "And our conference might be the worst in the nation, too. We might be the worst one double A team in the country."

"And VMI isn't even that good!" Jon seemed to agree, pointing out that Collin choked with his last interception and that Nick had two kicks blocked. To top it off, VMI racked up nearly 400 yards of offense against us.

"Yeah, but they were pretty hyped to play us," Mish said. "But, you're right Keeb, if we play like that it's possible we lose all our conference games."

Their pessimism was only half true, they said the words, but didn't fully mean them. Their timing, however, was completely inappropriate. Nobody on the bus wanted to hear that kind of talk, we would get enough of that from the media. Unfortunately, they had a way of verbalizing our deepest fears; we might not have what it takes.

Most of the guys plugged their headphones back in and tried to find a position comfortable enough to fall asleep.

I lingered, listening to the arguments and criticisms. My two cents worth of optimism was not welcome in the conversation and my abilities were shelved for the season. I felt helpless on all accounts. Besides, their minds were obviously made up.

Coach Achuff turned and glared, forgoing words to let his piercing blue eyes send the message. He heard their conversation and he had had enough, it was finished. Oh, and by the way, practice is going to be miserable next week.

CHAPTER 26

PLAYERS ONLY

MONDAY, OCTOBER 10, 2005

NORTH CHARLESTON, SC

The Sabbath, not surprisingly on a Southern Baptist campus, was dedicated to rest for players and coaches alike. Sundays in the Quads were spent watching football, avoiding homework, and licking the wounds of the previous day's battle. Yesterday, there were hardly triumphs to speak of, only tragedies. Individually and collectively we were beat up. Guys like CJ, who had been nursing a torn labrum since the beginning of the season, were in desperate need of rest. Their commitment to the team didn't let them go to the doctor or even whine about it. They went to treatments and they played through the pain. Some, like CJ, played as much as they could before something physically broke and they'd take a quick break before going back into the game. The bye week was in clear sight, two weeks away, and it couldn't get here soon enough.

Through the plexiglass of the weight room I watched the Athletic Training Center bustle like Grand Central Station. Toby jumped from athlete to athlete, diagnosing progress and directing traffic. Over in the corner, Andy used the ultrasound machine to sooth a hamstring back to health. Athletic training students filled ice bags and applied heating pads on various body parts. Nobody liked treatments this early in the morning, but 6 a.m. was the only time available in our busy schedules.

We lifted once per week. The body could only handle so much and the time available to do so was limited. The clang and bang of the 45-pound plates echoed throughout the weight room on my side of the plexiglass. I lifted, albeit a limited amount because of the healing hand, with the travel squad because the coaches wanted me on the sidelines during the games. I felt more like a coach than a player. I observed the team and spent time with them, yet I could not put on pads and I could not share their burdens. Even my workouts limited me to weightless squats, long rides on the stationary bike, and one-armed dumbbell bench presses – activities they'd never participate in.

Below the "BUCCANEER STRENGTH" printed in bold, blue letters across the cinder block walls, teammates squatted and bench pressed in the weight racks without enthusiasm. Obligatory sweat began to form on our yellow workout shirts and on our brows, but the weight room was devoid of energy. Coach Kelly sipped his first 32oz Diet Coke of the day in the corner of the weight room by the door, studying the room. The permanently tanned skin of his long forehead wrinkled up and he could sense that we felt sorry for ourselves. Between the lift and routine conditioning that followed, he stopped us in the hall for a pep talk.

Chuck Kelly, a hellfire and brimstone type of man, loved two things in this world: God and Football. In that order. He could crawl under your skin in a flash, but he'd be the first one to put his hand on you in prayer. As the oldest member of the coaching staff and the offensive line coach, he was the Indian Chief who had fought in more wars than the rest of the tribe. He had accumulated more experience than all of us put together.

Coach Kelly could see what we were going through. He understood what the dedication of the season meant and just as he believed in Jesus, he believed we could finish this season the way we wanted: with rings on our fingers. He knew Eddie well and he was just as passionate about the season as any of us. Without raising his voice, without making a scene, and without preaching the gospel, Coach Kelly spoke to us very clearly.

"Men, the season isn't lost," his Mississippi drawl gave his words soul. "We can still win this for Eddie. Now pick your heads up and let's go out to work. We can't win if we're feeling sorry for ourselves."

Conditioning, though plenty grueling for a pre-sunrise workout, sped by. Coach Kelly triggered something. Something that helped us through the week and inspired a players-only meeting in the Gold Room above the cafeteria. Position groups occasionally met without their coaches: defensive backs for film, linemen for food, etc. But a team meeting sans coaches had yet to take place this season. Captains closing the doors and getting real with teammates wasn't unexpected or uncommon given our situation. But what wasn't certain was the type of outcome it would produce.

The best leaders could take advantage of the stage and inspire their teams to achieve greatness. I had heard them speak before in years prior about passion for the game, pride in their uniforms, and how they cared about the team. They spoke about the sacrifices we had gone through as a unit and they would let emotions flow if they had to. They would bare their souls and they would be rewarded with renewed commitment from the group.

But, not everyone who stood up in front of their teams was a leader and their words could easily have the reverse effect on the team. They would hurry through a clichéd speech about how much *they* sacrificed, how much *they* wanted this, how much *they* were upset at the outcome of the season. Not everyone was cut out for public speaking. Or leadership for that matter.

I had no idea what to expect when the floor opened. A few guys talked about pride in what we were doing. Some talked about sacrifice, how they'd left their homes to come win here, not lose. Others talked about X's and O's and executing schemes. Much of their words were recycled and rephrased mantras we'd heard since we played pee wee ball. They were losing us. The meeting had the potential to be derailed by whining and pointing the finger of blame at the coaches or the lack of fans or the lack of perceived support from the school.

Shawn Huntsinger, the starting center was bold enough to say something controversial. Something that warranted the coaches leaving the room for him to say. Something that stuck.

"Screw the coaches, it's not about them," he said. "We're losing because we're not playing together. Because we're not playing hard. They can give us perfect schemes and if we don't play, it doesn't matter. It's on us to save this season, not anybody else. The coaches don't matter, the fans don't matter, the media doesn't matter. What matters are the guys in this room."

Maybe it was Shawn's statement or Coach Kelly's pick me up that caused us to pull together. Whatever the reason, the West Virginia Wesleyan Bobcats felt the full firepower of our offense the following Saturday. Last year we learned to compete. In the early part of this season we saw our own potential. Against the Bobcats, by way of 695 yards of total offense, we learned how to finish.

CHAPTER 27

BYE WEEK BASE CAMP

TUESDAY, OCTOBER 25, 2005

NORTH CHARLESTON, SC

"To get what you've never had, you must do what you'd never done."

The little piece of paper fell from the Hallmark card onto the blue rug of my dorm room floor. The heavy metal door closed behind me and I sat alone in the cinder block room on the edge of my twin bed reading the curly, elaborate letters of Mom's handwriting. She always knew when to send me inspirational quotes and motivational clippings. I must have made it pretty obvious I was feeling down when we spoke Friday before the game, she sent stuff like this when she thought I was in need of a boost.

After my surgery I was a bit delusional. Not from the pain killers, but from my own desire to finish the season. Sitting on the sideline week in and week out crushed me. Okeba wasn't playing bad and we won our last two games, but I wasn't content being a bystander. My competitive nature wouldn't let me be content. Alone in my dorm with nothing but my self-pity, I unloaded my Accounting 101 books onto the small wooden desk.

The docs told me I had an outside chance to play in eight to 10 weeks, so naturally I made it a goal to play in six weeks. Today marked week eight. Coach Mills had no desire to waste a medical redshirt year for me and Toby Harkins, the head athletic trainer, was still concerned about my safety. He let me ride the stationary bike and perform limited workouts, but just last week he scolded me for jumping in ball drills while, I thought, he wasn't looking.

I finally let go of delusion and realized that I wouldn't play again until next season. I dipped my toe in the deep end of a pool of bitterness, as Mom could tell, but I resigned to keep a positive attitude and do my best to support the team any way I could. I could still be with them at all times, be a teacher to Okeba and the other guys, be an assistant to Coach Perkins, provide encouragement, anything the team needed. I knew these were important for a team's health, but that's not how I wanted to contribute. I would gladly trade a year of eligibility and my personal health for a chance to put on pads tomorrow – even if it was just practice. That lust for battle was amplified 10-fold on game day.

My thoughts drifted from personal woes to the past two Saturdays while I got ready for bed. Our offense had scored over 100 points in the last two games. The Division 2 West Virginia Wesleyan Bobcats gave us more of a fight than we bargained for, putting up 48 of their own points in an offensive shootout that lasted way too long. The following week Savannah State only scored 28 points compared to our 48, but that was enough to make us question what we had been doing on defense. We beat both teams, but not without our own bumps and bruises. We won both games, but they were hardly dominating performances.

The upcoming game with Gardner Webb would be the biggest one of the season, so far. I wondered if we could keep that sort of offensive pace. I wondered about that out-of-place warning the coaches shared yesterday in the team meeting about the Safe Harbor drug testing program. I wondered if some of our defensive weaknesses would be exposed when we played a more equipped

Collin Drafts (7) and the offensive line aim for one of six
offensive touchdowns against Savannah State in the south endzone.

opponent.

Mills, who seemed to have a crystal ball for the future,
scheduled our bye week perfectly. We headed into our off week
with confidence and a chance to recuperate from the first eight
games of the season. Our next three games consisted of the best
opponents in the conference, seeded one, two, and three in
preseason rankings. We had 11 days to prepare for Gardner Webb's
high powered offense, ranked among the tops in 1-AA football.
If we didn't win this game, our dreams of a championship would
never be fulfilled. But, it didn't stop there. We had to win this week,
and the week after that, and the week after that to be the champs.
If the Big South trophy was the summit, we had three successively
higher mountains ahead of us to scale. All we could do for the next
11 days was sit here at base camp and stare up at the peaks that
waited for us, mentally and physically preparing ourselves for the

challenges we were about to face.

– – – *Tuesday, November 1, 2005* – – –

Cool air blasted through the vents of the locker room, circulating the stench of dried sweat. Each stained wooden locker was perfectly arranged with helmets on the left and shoulder pads on the right as Coach Kelly, humming some nameless gospel, moved laboriously across the thin blue carpet tossing laundry bags into corresponding lockers.

"So apparently they were tipped off by a player?" I asked only half-rhetorically, slumping down in a locker next to Collin.

"Yep, hard to believe," said Collin. Like most of us, he knew we could survive without them, but this seemed like an unnecessary hurdle. His frustration took physical form as he shoved his knee pads into his pants for practice with extra force.

"That's Mills for ya," Reggie chimed in with clichéd pessimism. "Coulda just let it go, but he wanted to set a precedent."

The locker room was unusually quiet. Not because of a lack of players, just a lack of conversation. The topic had already been exhausted. News spread fast about the events of the past week. Events that, in hindsight, we should have seen coming. The ominous warning about the Safe Harbor drug testing program all made sense now. Coach Mills received an "anonymous" tip from a concerned senior player that a number of our teammates were in need of drug testing. Coach Mills, being a moral man, followed through with the lead and initiated the largest round of drug testing imaginable. A few clean players like Shawn Huntsinger, the starting center, were sprinkled in to give it the illusion of a random testing. We knew better. As soon as Shawn reported to testing, as he later told me, "I knew a few of 'em were done." Four of our 10 seniors were immediately dismissed from the team.

The senior pruning wasn't the end of the unraveling. A starting junior defensive lineman was involved in a fight downtown, something Mills and the university were forced to punish with dismissal from the team. Although we witnessed the police escort him from the practice field in full pads, it became official, he would not be welcomed back.

Finally, with what some might call ironic justice, the senior who called in the anonymous tip for drug use was caught up in something extracurricular on campus. We didn't receive all the details, only his pleas for us to sign a petition to let him back on the team. But the school would have none of it. His petition was rejected by a school council and he, too, was off the team.

After the six players were dismissed, the mayhem dissipated. Coaches remained optimistic about the situation, calling the exodus a "trimming of the fat" and referencing scripture about punishment for deeds done wrong. We couldn't drop our teammates as swiftly. We still lived in the dorms with them. We still saw them in the cafeteria morning, noon, and night. Our history of groggy mornings and sweaty afternoons alongside them wasn't going away overnight.

The scandals weren't being audibly discussed as I moved down between Okeba and Eddie's old locker to mine. Today marked a new day, one that would set us back on our weekly routine. Although minds raced, bodies had been rested.

Knowing no amount of complaining would change the events of the past week, teammates laced up cleats and strapped on shoulder pads with stoic resolve. We couldn't do anything about the dismissals. Each player who was kicked off was in control of their own destiny and each made decisions they knew could land them in trouble. Wasting energy debating the events that had transpired was pointless; all we could do was push forward. We cared about the guys who had been dismissed, but we didn't have time to lament their loss; we had a game in four days. No matter what decisions were made, we knew no single individual was bigger than the team or the mission.

After a flawless practice that afternoon, a cold, somewhat calloused feeling followed us back into the locker room. Maybe we wouldn't miss them at all.

To view more images from the Savannah State game, go to http://BelieveEG21.com/ssu

CHAPTER 28

GARDNER WEBB UNIVERSITY

SATURDAY, NOVEMBER 5, 2005

BOILING SPRINGS, NC

My breath fogged the window of the charter bus as I watched the oranges, reds, and yellows of fall from the road. I could allow myself to be distracted, my game day preparation wasn't as intense as my teammates' in the seats surrounding me. Their headphones canceled the hum of the bus engine and they were lost in visualizations of the pending conflict they were about to take part in.

Eyes shifted from the trees to the front of the bus when Coach Barrows stood and motioned for everyone to remove their headphones. With an earnest and firm voice, he reminded us how hard we had worked since the spring. He reminded us of how we had been humbled since we started the season so cocky. He reminded us that this season was dedicated to Eddie Gadson, whose father would be in the stands that afternoon.

"Men, today you gotta believe. Believe in yourselves. Believe in each other. Believe in the offense and special teams and in each other and the coaching staff. Believe that you can be champs!"

Heads nodded and eyes locked on the small screens scattered across the roof of the bus. Coach Perkins discretely popped in a video tape while Barrows stood before us in the aisle of the bus with his signature gray coaching sweatshirt that read "BUCCANEER FOOTBALL" across the chest. A blank screen gave way to our cutlass and Al Pacino's husky voice broke the silence. The famous pre-game monologue from "Any Given Sunday," a team favorite, had been dubbed over a highlight reel from the first half of the season. The tape flashed big hits by the linebackers, interceptions by the DB's, and sacks by the D-line.

Pacino talked about healing or being defeated. He talked about being kicked and taking it or doing something about our situation. His dialogue matched up perfectly to our mindset. Time to bicker about who we'd lost on this journey had passed. If we didn't do something drastic and come together today, our season would be over. The seemingly endless number of plays on the tape inspired confidence in our abilities. We possessed the ability to make plays, but we never seemed to believe in ourselves the way the coaches did.

Pacino's voice grew stronger over the bus speakers. Sacrifice. Team. Fight.

We had the ability to be a championship team if, and only if, we pulled together. The only way to do it was by believing in each other, believing that the men on the bus were the ones we could count on to give it their all in every situation.

Today was the biggest battle of our careers. If we didn't win today, we would be out of the race for the championship. We had three opponents left and we needed to beat all three. This might as well have been playoffs. Without a win today, a championship was all but impossible.

Pacino's speech closed perfectly with the highlights and we exited the bus to catch up with the offense. As each man stepped off, Coach Barrows, Coach Perkins, and Coach Achuff gave a fist bump and a reminder to "believe" as we headed toward the visitor's locker room.

— — —

Sometime during the first half, on a dry erase board in big black marker, Coach Barrows wrote "B-E-L-I-E-V-E" for everyone to see. Both times Okeba had pass breakups and then again when he had a tackle for loss, Barrows thrust the sign upwards from the sideline. Okeba's self-applied pressure was paying off. Today was homecoming for Okeba. He got to play in front of his family from Gastonia, North Carolina, just a few miles up I-85. It marked the first time his family had seen him play in a Buccaneer jersey and he wanted nothing less than to make them gush with pride, a feeling every one of us was familiar with.

A freshman named Tyrese Harris, who had replaced one of the players lost in the commotion of the past few weeks, was making tackles all over the field. He also received the marker board recognition. When David Misher intercepted a pass, Barrows shoved the marker board in his face as a greeting back on the sideline. The offense not only received the marker board treatment from Barrows, but from the rest of the defense as they put up 28 points in the first two quarters.

The offensive line, which had not given up a sack all day, kept Collin's jersey clean. With almost no exceptions, they also kept the running backs moving forward. After a year of simmering, they had become the perfect concoction of tenured JUCO transfers and talented second-year players. Like an expedition into a remote land, supplies were limited this season. Due to injuries and a shallow depth chart, only seven offensive lineman had seen significant playing time this season. But they weren't upset, Coach Kelly had been preparing them for it since spring ball. The mandatory group meals helped them figure out each other's personalities. All the duck walks across the field, crouched low with their hands on their heads, were paying off in stamina. The 6:00 a.m. workouts he forced them to attend as a unit made more sense, they worked well together.

DeAndre Harrison, the right tackle who could down 10 bowls of pasta during all-you-can-eat-night at Olive Garden, was quiet for a senior. He preferred to show leadership instead of talk about it.

Sophomore Rick Howell was an offensive linemen we were glad to have on our team. He was thick, powerful, and possessed a savage attitude that flourished under the pile. He was known to run downfield, in practice and in games, to "pick off" anyone standing around the pile with seemingly unwarranted vengeance; a habit that placed him in the center of numerous scuffles with me, CJ, and anyone wearing a defensive jersey. Though his licks sometimes felt like a cheap shot in practice, we loved to watch him work during games.

Senior Shawn Huntsinger, literally and proverbially the center of the offensive line, had permanently sacrificed his body to the game. His right ring finger was broken so badly it jutted outwards 45 degrees at the first knuckle. His leadership on the O-line helped Collin determine fronts and make checks. His words about playing hard for each other, not the coaches or fans or anyone else, helped spark the team to the last two wins during our players only meeting three weeks prior. Considered one of the best centers in the conference despite his deformity, Shawn's game was as mentally taxing as it was physical.

Alex Bragg's brand new black, jacked up GMC Sierra 2500 pickup truck was what the O-line would go muddin' in. The country boy from Augusta was the strong silent type as well, coming into his own as a guard this season.

Troy James, only slightly less obnoxious than Howell, was just as tough of a lineman. He, like many players who suited up, was held together with an assortment of braces and athletic tape on game day. Before the season he had been ready to hang up his cleats and retire after only one year. But Huntsinger, one of his best friends off the field, wouldn't let him. Adjectives like "indispensable" flattered James enough to buy into Huntsinger's pleas and stick out his sophomore year.

Rounding out the starting offensive line was the final JUCO transfer, Bryan Meers. Though only a tight end, he was one of the most technically sound and dependable blockers on the field. He was the kind of player who saw the value of hard work and held his teammates to the same standard, calling them out if they wavered. He was the kind of player who wrote a private sticky note on Mills' door apologizing for his lack of focus and that, "you can count on me to be the player and leader you've been seeking."

Normally, this offensive line gave Coach Kelly a daily aneurysm. Jumping offside would cause him to throw haymakers into the air with a fury that could cause a freshman to transfer. Missed assignments on film would stifle meetings so badly he could only work through three plays in an hour. Today, there were less harsh words. No shadow boxing took place and no dry erase markers were punched through marker boards out of frustration, the offensive line held their own. Safe until Monday's film session.

Collin made risky throws on plays like "Five Seattle." A play in which receivers mirror corner routes to their respective sidelines to pull the safeties from the middle of the field, the running back's destination. The running back wasn't his read, and he wasn't technically open, but Collin threw it anyway. Perfection! God or Eddie or something was guiding us better than we could have done ourselves.

At halftime we found ourselves staring out the open door of the locker room to Spangler Stadium. The afternoon air had warmed as the sun cast long shadows over the sunken valley of the stadium. Homecoming balloons jerked in the breeze on the fences surrounding the stadium like red and black bumble bees. The stands, dug out of the orange clay that formed the ground of southwest North Carolina, remained still though they were filled with onlookers. They were stunned.

Coach Mills reiterated the points from his pre-game speech about Michael Jordan never taking his eye off the ball and the concentration required to finish a game such as this. He commended guys like Okeba, David Misher and the freshman Tyrese.

This game could be typical for CSU. In years past, we would not have had the gall to finish a game such as this. We would cave in on ourselves and the team would coast into a sub-par finish to the season. Expectations from the outside world were not high. Just like years prior, we were mathematically in the hunt for the championship, only having lost one conference game. But this wasn't years past, and outside expectations didn't matter inside this locker room. Today, we believed.

We should have been a team without depth, having lost players to injuries and stupid decisions. We should have been a team that rolled over for Gardner Webb. That's what they expected, at least. Before the game began, 30 minutes of game clock earlier, both teams were mathematically in the hunt for a championship.

Coach Mills used his signature line, "What the mind can conceive, the body can achieve." Emotion infiltrated his voice, he was still unsure if this was a dream.

The Gardner Webb stands were in shock because they hadn't expected this Buccaneer team, who let two Division 2 teams combine for 84 points and a win against them, hold their top five nationally ranked scoring offense to zero points, gaining less than 100 yards. The Charleston Southern stands were in shock because they'd never seen us play with such ferocity. We didn't drop a pass, we didn't take a loss on any snap during the first half. We pushed forward like a Spartan army pushing back their enemies, one unified step at a time. On offense, drives of 86, 78, 80, and 65 yards had all resulted in points. The Gardner Webb special teams unit erased our hopes of a shutout with a 76-yard punt return up the sideline. The idea of a shutout against GWU was hard to fathom. But the punt return turned out to be the only mistake of the day; now, at halftime, we led the Runnin' Bulldogs 28-7.

Mills broke the huddle on "FINISH!" as we stepped out into the afternoon sun to put our opponents out of their misery. The

Runnin' Bulldogs, just as we were when the game began, were still mathematically in this game. Unfortunately for them, math had nothing to do with the momentum at our backs.

Late in the third quarter Okeba, who was playing his best game since he took over for me, intercepted a pass at the 15 yard line on first down. Exhausted, he attempted to fall down as soon as the intended receiver nabbed his jersey from behind. Helmets of black and of gold swarmed around him attempting to will him toward opposite endzones. Both opponents and teammates, like CJ, attempted to strip him of the ball. He let his legs go limp and gave in to the influence of the scrum as it slowly imploded. When the pile of bodies was peeled away, Okeba lay in the endzone with our final score of the day. His coming out party in front of family gave him the confidence he longed for since Jacksonville University. In his mind, he had earned his spot amongst the starters with today's performance.

The defense and the team hadn't fallen apart without me. Okeba's play humbled me and put my ego in check. I wasn't bigger than the team, nobody was. The past two weeks were evidence of that fact. Through the injury, I learned what it felt like to surrender to the group. I thought I'd be bitter, but the feeling never came. Standing on the sideline still dressed in my travel clothes as we thumped Gardner Webb, I felt more a part of the team than ever.

A certain amount of luck seems to follow winning teams. Receivers caught passes they shouldn't have. Defenders made tackles that seemed improbable. But, today had little to do with luck; we played our best, most complete game of the season. We outplayed Gardner Webb in every facet of the game despite penalties, dismissed players, and the tear-jerking pressure of knowing that today was a must-win if we were to keep our championship hopes alive.

Fans who had journeyed to Boiling Springs to see us play greeted us with smiles and hugs as we eased triumphantly off the field with a 38-7 victory. We had just delivered Gardner Webb their lowest point total of the season and their first loss to our program. In no rush to forget this moment, Coach Mills let us take an extra few minutes with our meager fan base before packing up the travel buses and heading home.

Fans and parents like Ed Gadson sent abundant, joyous cheers of, "Two more of those ought to do the trick!" They knew this victory would keep our hopes of a conference championship in plain sight. We held their offense, who had averaged nearly 40 points per game, to a single touchdown. Beating a notable conference opponent by 31 points was no accident, something special was happening. Unfortunately, that meant we'd no longer be the underdog. Like a special forces team whose cover was blown, we wouldn't be able to sneak up on anyone after this win.

Administrators like Christie Faircloth Dixon were more conservative with their congratulatory words. They knew the next challenge was nothing like Gardner Webb or any team we had played all season. The Liberty University Flames were the most well-funded, winningest football program in the Big South Conference. They were able to recruit some of the largest, most physical players in 1-AA each year, regularly stealing a handful from big time programs like Virginia Tech and Pitt. The administration knew what was invested in this season and they knew how much of a heartbreak a loss would be. They had seen us win and they had seen our transformation, but they knew the mountain of a task, literally and physically, ahead of us was unlike anything we had previously scaled. They were happy for us. But it was the kind of cautious optimism a parent shows when they don't want to get their child's hopes up too high for fear of failure.

The hum of the bus wheels was drowned out by joyous conversation for the three-hour ride home. Gardner Webb was the last away game of the season. Liberty would come to us in seven days. But the Flames were the last thing on our minds, we cherished the satisfaction of this victory. We needed the boost of confidence that came with this sort of accomplishment. We needed some confidence back now that we knew how to use it.

In any pair of seats you could hear detailed conversations about blitzes that almost didn't work and plays that were barely made. Al Pacino quotes swirled through the bus and the coaches shared a grin. Two more to go.

CHAPTER 29

LIBERTY UNIVERSITY

SATURDAY, NOVEMBER 12, 2005

NORTH CHARLESTON, SC

Campus was still as I made the long trek from the stadium back to the locker room. Organizing the defensive bench was a perfect excuse to pull myself from the magnitude of the locker room. I couldn't bare the quiet, I wanted to skip to the ensuing anarchy.

The perfect 55-degree morning was just mild enough for a thin mist to cover the pond outside of the locker room like bubbles over a freshly poured soft drink. The Charleston Choke had long ceased to be present; natural elements were no longer a parlor trick we could depend on for an upper hand. Our only advantage was that we didn't have to travel eight hours in a bus the day prior like our opponents. The field behind me was freshly painted for game day. Orange pylons outlined the corners of the endzone and goal post pads reading "CSU" bookended the field under the yellow goal posts. The stadium still echoed with an instrumental version of The Game's "Hate it or love it," the closest thing the Southern Baptist school would allow to pre-game music.

The air on the field, hushed and cool, matched the air in the locker room as I stepped back through the double doors. Focused teammates readied their equipment for the game.

Cleats: inspected and cleaned with damp paper towels. Tube socks: adjusted to fit comfortably, peaking just above the ankle braces or tape. Helmets: wiped fresh from the scars earned during practice. Mills' rules about not wearing wrist or sweatbands left arms bare other than taped wrists. Baggy jerseys were tucked into every possible crevice, even if only to start the game, whether in waist bands or shoulder pads.

Determining whether calm mornings translate to nervousness, preparation, intimidation, or any combination of these is nearly impossible until kickoff. The entire week of practice had been calm and focused like this, something the coaches recognized and for which we were rewarded. Coach Perkins called it a "business trip" as he explained the reasons for lodging us in a clean hotel the night before - no distractions, bigger beds, and to treat us like the winners they knew us to be.

The coaches shared the administrators' sentiments after our win against Gardner Webb, cautioning us about getting ahead of ourselves. Coach Mills reiterated the mantra that, "Nothing is as good as it seems, and nothing is as bad as it seems. The film tells all." And it did. We played good against Gardner Webb, but not perfect. They exposed special teams weaknesses and our lack of discipline. When tallied, we accumulated over 100 yards in avoidable penalties.

All week Coach Barrows compared our win against Gardner Webb to the shortcomings against The Citadel. "B-E-L-I-E-V-E," was written in big bold letters on our game plans. Barrows chanted it every day at practice, never letting us forget why or how we had won with such dominance.

As kickoff ticked closer, the business-like atmosphere remained intact. Coach Mills, with a slight forced frown on his face, reminded us where we came from in his pre-game speech. He too was ready for battle in his blue visor, pressed khaki pants, and white shirt adorned with only the CSU cutlass and the black "EG21" dot on opposing sleeves. He reminded us we had outworked Liberty, we were more disciplined, we had overcome more obstacles, and that we were better conditioned. He urged us to remember where we came from, that the fresh linens of the Comfort Suites the night before were a first for this program. In his mind's eye, he saw the floral prints of the dingy hotel room in Jacksonville where he had dropped to his knees in prayer years before; so much ground had been covered since then.

"Some teams have substance and some teams have style," he continued. "We have substance. We have learned to play together over the course of this season. Most importantly, we have learned to win together! We have learned to believe in each other! Men, we don't need to do anything different, just better. Success is when opportunity meets preparation. I have no doubt in my mind that the team in front of me is prepared for victory today!"

Invincible. The attitude wasn't premeditated or talked about. It just was. No matter how many Proverbs Coach Mills quoted, the team ego was difficult to turn off. He said it himself, we were in a position to achieve significant accomplishments. But nobody was going to give it to us, we had to earn it.

Our first drive against the Liberty Flames started strong, battling for nine plays over 63 yards. Collin orchestrated the offense with ease, connecting on short passes from the pocket and scrambling for a few yards when he didn't like his reads. Four minutes into the game we led 7-0, just as expected. The defense, led by Degraf and the freshman Tyrese Harris, put a stop to Liberty's first drive around mid-field where they were forced to punt.

Depending on your side of the field, back to back thuds are the worst sound a special teams coach can hear. Blocked punts swing momentum like no other play in football. They force a turnover, demoralize the opponent, and often result in a score. The blocked punt is a rare, but important occurrence. It injects a shot of adrenaline into the vein of the blocking team and sucks the life out of the other just as fast.

THUD-THUD

The Flames seemed to be foaming at the mouth to get back in the endzone when we heard the sound. We were on the losing side of the kick. We had been pinned on our 10-yard line after Liberty punted to us. Collin and the offense couldn't get out from under the Flames suffocating defense and we were forced to punt after three short plays. We recovered the blocked punt inside our own endzone. The Flames earned two points and the ball was back in their possession after a free kick. Momentum swung their way.

Fortunately, the Flames used all their energy on the blocked punt and gave us the ball back quickly. Unfortunately, their punter pinned us inside our own 15-yard line. The Buccaneer offense needed an 85-yard excursion against the rabid Flame defense to put another touchdown on the board.

Mills and Collin both knew they needed a big play. Ever since Eddie passed, his duties had been filled by committee. Murry stepped in for short, tough passes. Rucks helped stretch the field. Meers had even helped as an outlet in situations. But Maurice Price had stepped up to take the role of big-time-playmaker. Collin hit him on first and 10 on the ensuing offensive series, giving him plenty of room to get upfield on a bubble screen toward the Liberty sideline. 73 yards later, we extended our lead to 15-2. The cheat sheet flopping from the front of Coach Mills' khakis told him a two-point conversion was the correct technical move for the situation. He opted for a two point conversion, another pass to Price, instead of an extra point in case the game came down to a single score. Fingers crossed that wouldn't happen.

In the papers and across radio broadcasts, similarities to the two squads had been drawn. Surface level observations like "young but talented," and "not sure how to finish," were frequently used by commentators. Liberty had played in tight games, just as we had, losing to Gardner Webb and VMI by less than eight total points and to Coastal in a triple overtime shootout.

The physical similarities to Liberty were non-existent. Our quick hit offense and speed-driven defense were the opposite of their size and strategy. Their offense was powered by a strong running game and mammoth-sized offensive linemen, some of whom transferred from larger programs. They played their game well, mixing in effective play-action passes after a heavy dose of pounding run plays. Play-action, faking a running play while intending to pass, was how they dropped a 64-yard bomb of a touchdown pass on us just before the first quarter ran out.

Despite the fact that we gave up an average of 30 pounds per lineman, our front was holding their own. A mid-season adjustment came after our defensive ends begged and pleaded with Coaches Achuff and Mills to let the ends angle them inwards instead of perpendicular to the line of scrimmage. The adjustment seemed to be paying off; Degraf, Harris, and our other ends like Stonewall Randolph III seemed to make it to the backfield every series. It was only a matter of time before they started making plays.

Every play the ball seemed to end up in the hands of Liberty's running back Zach Terrell, who ran hard between the tackles, or quarterback Brock Smith, who played a less disciplined version of Collin's mobile game. Four yards from Terrell backed up by a 17-yard completion by Smith. Four-yard run, 11-yard completion. Two more passes and Liberty found the endzone for the second time. The Flames stole momentum and a touchdown as they constructed a 14-play drive spanning 80 yards just before halftime. They opted to kick an extra point and we went into half trailing by one point, 16-15.

Determination seemed to pump through the air ducts of the locker room. Sweating bodies took their places inside the wooden lockers and athletic trainers made rounds to cover up open wounds. Players and coaches alike discussed vivid accounts of the first half, detailing the successes and mistakes of each drive with objectivity. This wasn't Gardner Webb and we weren't going to blow out the Flames. On defense, we needed to keep the running game minimized and watch out for deep passes from Smith. On offense, Price needed the ball in his hands. No time for gambling or breaking from game plans, Liberty was hungry for a conference win and they could smell opportunity.

Liberty carried its momentum into the second half without looking back. They scored a touchdown within five minutes of starting the second half and again as we entered the fourth quarter. The only points we were able to muster came in the form of a field goal after we were stoned at the two yard line. We fell behind 30-18 with just over 12 minutes in the game. A loss today would end our championship hopes. Coastal was the only team left to play and they had yet to lose to a conference opponent.

But we weren't thinking about Coastal Carolina, or losing, or anything except the fake punt about to be attempted. Ever since the punt block in the first quarter Liberty dominated us. Smith threw crisp passes, Terrell fell forward with the ball, and with one exception their defense kept us off the scoreboard. They played with a confidence we hadn't seen since in person. The confidence bordered on arrogance, the same thing we struggled with early in the season. Coach Mills recognized the hubris and called "Magic," a fake punt that would put the ball in the hands of our playmaker.

Sidney Bryant, the backup quarterback unfortunate enough to enter the program one year after Collin, hustled into the game in an abnormal spot on the punt team, as a blocker. The quick snap sent the Liberty punt return unit into a tailspin of confusion. Helmets jerked left and right across the new formation as players assessed who to cover and how to line up. Bryant took a single step and dropped the ball into the numbers of Price's jersey for a 15 yard gain, more than enough for a first down.

With the fake punt we stole the first down and propelled the rest of the drive with enthusiasm. One quick slant to Price and two hard runs by Robert Adams got us into the endzone, 30-25 with less than 10:00 to go.

"This team is young and talented," quipped Jon Davis over the radio waves. "But, I don't know if they know how to finish a game." The unassigned comment applied to both sidelines.

The ensuing kickoff left the Flames pinned on their two-yard line after another booming kick. The Flames had obviously been rattled on the last series. A few safe play calls and a botched punt later, we resumed possession with 6:39 left to recover the lead and 55 yards of grass ahead of us. A field goal wouldn't work, we needed to score a touchdown.

The Liberty defense sagged as the realization settled on them that they hadn't, in fact, already won the game. Three first downs in a row was much faster than Mills had anticipated us driving. He was hoping to waste more of the clock and leave Liberty with mere seconds of possession after we scored. A series of forced scrambles by Collin and gashing zone runs by Dre put us six yards from paydirt. Collin tried to scramble in: fail. Dre tried to muscle in: fail. Collin tried a quick toss to Meers: fail. Fourth and goal from the four yard line. Mills needed to convene with his coaches on the headset and his quarterback in person.

"Timeout!" Mills said to the closest guy in the zebra suit.

Maurice Price was one of the most naturally gifted players to ever wear a CSU cutlass. He was a tall, lean receiver with sub 4.4 40-yard dash speed and 40-plus inch vertical leap. His central Florida roots gave him something to brag about; he was a stand-out in one of the largest schools in the state before his accomplishments at CSU had begun to pile up. He was a completely different player than Eddie Gadson in stature, but he was learning to fill the void Eddie left with his own set of unique talents. Nobody was going to outrun him if the pass was thrown deep and nobody was going to out jump him if the ball was thrown up in the air. Although our offense wasn't made for a deep threat like Price, he was a standout. He frequently turned short bubble screens in 30-yard plays after getting the ball in his hands and was a no-brainer if we needed someone to go get a ball in the air. Which is exactly what Mills had in mind on fourth and goal from the four-yard line.

With 2:53 on the clock, Collin, from the shotgun formation, took a single step and lobbed a pass to Price in the corner of the endzone. The ball's velocity was slow but the spiral was tight. The nose of the ball turned over at the peak of the ball's arc and it descended rapidly toward Price's hands.

2,500 fans locked their eyes on the southwest corner of the endzone. We came off the bench and crowded the sideline to get a better view of the show Price was about to put on. Bodies leaned over each other and all heads pointed in one direction. This was our last chance, the outcome of our season hung in the air.

As the ball fell, Price and two Liberty defenders sprung upwards with hands outstretched. They knew he was going to be the target the second he lined up wide. The dog fight in mid-air proved fruitless and Price came down empty handed.

Heads bobbed forward and palms went skyward in protest, "They were all over him!"

The far sideline judge agreed with our pleas and he reached for the yellow flag in his belt loop. The pass interference call awarded us a fresh set of four downs from the two-yard line.

First down and goal from the two: Dre got lost in a mixed sea of red, white, and blue jerseys.

Second and goal from the two: the pressure of the situation mounted and Alex Bragg jumped offside.

"Seriously?" Collin hollered in disbelief. All he could do was laugh. Bragg knew he messed up, he didn't need a lecture. Collin wasn't usually this loose, but something had come over him earlier in the drive. On a broken play, "Lazy Sticks," he turned a potential sack into a 19-yard run on third and 12. Ever since, he knew he couldn't do wrong. We had come too far to blow it. "Let's tighten up fellas, almost there! Let's put this one away!" He let his teammates see his smile and his relaxed attitude spoke more to his teammates than his words ever could.

On the sideline, Mills didn't want to keep gambling this game away. His eyes aimlessly scanned the play call sheet flopped over his belt loop. He knew who the ball should go to.

Third and 10 from the two: incomplete bubble pass to Price. We had somehow found ourselves in worse field position than before the pass interference call. With 1:16 on the clock, we used our last timeout to regroup. We hadn't gained ground for six consecutive plays and Liberty seemed to find a second wind along with a sixth sense for where the ball was headed. The pass interference call bailed us out last time, we couldn't count on lightning striking twice for another set of downs, this was our final chance to take back the lead.

Mills' deliberation with Collin was short. "Gun Trey Left - Rip Two Milk - Green." Collin cracked a smile, the ever-humble Jay Mills had been infected with a dose of our ego.

Rucks, Murry, and Meers split left, leaving Price by himself as the sole receiver on the right side of the formation. From the shotgun, Collin barked for the snap. No need to feign going left, everyone on the field and in the stands knew who was going to get the ball.

Price stutter-stepped inside on a slant then broke quickly upfield into the endzone to complete the double move. He was wedged between the cornerback outside of him and the safety who had come over from his high inside position. Maurice Price and the defending cornerback bounded into the air. Price's body climbed higher and higher until his hands reached above the goal post crossbar and his feet dangled around the waist of the Flame. The cornerback pulled at his baggy jersey and leaned into Price's frame in an attempt to throw the receiver off balance in mid-air. The defender was in perfect position but nothing he did could stop the raw athleticism of a 41-inch vertical leap. A second Flame defender came to the party late and unsuccessfully tried to knock the ball loose. Price

Maurice Price (1) makes his 13th catch of the game. The catch added Price's name to the record books alongside Eddie Gadson's for most catches in a game and delivered our program its first victory over Liberty.

landed on top of the opposing players with the ball secure in his hands. 31–30, Buccaneers.

A failed two-point conversion would have put us up by three and would have forced Liberty to at least kick a field goal to force an overtime. We didn't need it. The young Flames team panicked and failed to get past their own 35-yard line after another deep kick.

After the game, Mills' faith provoked him to share his devotional from Os Hillman regarding our recent victories.

"The second son he named Ephraim and said, 'It is because God has made me fruitful in the land of my suffering.'" Genesis 41:52

Whenever God takes us through the land of affliction, He will do two things through that affliction: First, He will bring such healing that we will be able to forget the pain, and second He will make us fruitful from the painful experiences.

God does not waste our afflictions if we allow Him the freedom to complete the work in us. His desire is to create virtue that remains during the times of testing so that He can bring us into the place of fruitfulness in the very area of our testing. He has never promised to keep us from entering the valleys of testing, but He has promised to make us fruitful in them.

This wasn't the team who lost to the Citadel. This wasn't the team who was blown out by Presbyterian. This was a new team. A team that had just earned its first winning season in the 14-year history of sanctioned games for the program. A team who had endured affliction and a team who now believed. A team who had resolved to finish what it started.

"Men, enjoy the fruits of your labor. Because next Saturday, November 19th, we play for a conference championship!"

To view more images from the Liberty game, go to http://BelieveEG21.com/liberty

CHAPTER 30

COASTAL CAROLINA UNIVERSITY

SATURDAY, NOVEMBER 19, 2005

NORTH CHARLESTON, SC

"Men, back in October we said only two teams controlled their own destinies. And we're meeting in a few hours for the title." Coach Mills' voice shook with energy. He wasn't thinking about the players he asked to leave the team just weeks before. He wasn't debating whether or not the added expense of the hotel rooms last night was worth paying. The only thing he was concerned with were the men in the room gingerly eating breakfast. He studied every one of us in the room as we quietly ate small mounds of bacon, eggs, syrup-covered pancakes, cereal, and fruit.

"I see a team driven by an unquenchable desire for victory. A team whose end result is hoisting up a Big South Championship trophy. But a lot needs to happen between now and then. We must be physically and mentally tougher than our opponent, and we must play with the heart of a champion as well, too." His voice remained steady but we inched to the edge of our seats with anticipation.

Besides the Big South logo on the helmets, the two schools shared little. Coastal was known as a public party school outside a party city, Myrtle Beach. CSU was known as a private Southern Baptist school in the Holy City. Coastal Carolina, known as the reigning conference champs from the year prior. Charleston Southern, known as the dunce of the Big South, earning one conference victory in 11 years. With only four teams in the conference suiting up for football, each game held championship implications. But VMI, Gardner Webb, and Liberty called different states home. We considered Coastal Carolina, just two hours north, our most bitter rival.

"Coastal sees us as, and I quote, 'The doormat to the Big South Championship and their at-large bid to the 1 AA playoffs.' Huh…" Mills shook his head with a proud, but disagreeing nod as he pulled out a stat sheet from his back pocket. "I think they need glasses, because men, here's what I see.

"I see the second best kickoff return unit in the league with an average of 20.2 yards per return. Ranked ahead of Coastal and the only team in the league to score a touchdown this season. I see a team whose punt return unit is the second leading unit in the conference with 11 yards per return. Coastal has no one ranked. I see a team who has been perfect for the last five weeks on field goals and extra points."

I glanced to my left at Nick Ellis as he clenched his teeth and nodded his head, graciously accepting the pat on the back I extended his way. "Nick we'll need you tomorrow, I don't know how or when, but I guarantee we will," Mills added.

"I see a team who is ranked number one in the Big South in rushing yards allowed, number 21 nationally, over the past four weeks of play. A defense who has only given up 22.75 points per game, number two in the Big South and number 41 nationally, over the past four weeks. A defense who is plus two point five in the turnover ratio in the last four games.

"I see a team who has cracked the top 20 in rushing offense

over the past four weeks, who has broken the top 10 in passing efficiency, a team whose total offense per game is over 450 yards! Good enough to be number three in the country over the past four weeks. A team who has scored 45 points per game over the past four weeks, good enough to be number one in the country for scoring offense." Mills folded his stat sheet and made eye contact with what seemed like everyone in the room. "That doesn't sound like a doormat to me."

"Coach Bennett from Coastal was quoted in the papers this week saying, 'This isn't the same CSU team we've faced in the past,' and I have to agree, we're not."

"Ephesians 5:33 talks about men needing respect. Men, we have not been given the respect we deserve. Not from Coastal, not from the media. I don't care if Coastal is 9-1. They may not know it yet, but a new king of the Big South is being crowned today!"

Cheers, whistles, and fist pumps filled the room as Mills bowed out of the most exciting pre-game speech he had ever delivered to us. We would ready to play in a few short hours.

– – –

The brisk afternoon sky was peppered with the occasional straggling cloud formation. The crisp air was just cool enough for spectators to justify long-sleeves. Behind me in the stands, Dad told my brother it was perfect football weather. The two of them hopped in the car just hours after his high school game, they wouldn't miss the chance to see us compete for a championship. Mom and a handful of family members on her side also made the four-hour journey from Jacksonville to see the game. Although there was zero chance I'd play, they supported me in any way they could. They knew how important the game was to me. They'd known it all season. Between Mom and Dad, someone attended nearly every home game despite my lack of participation.

Anticipation flooded Charleston Southern University's campus as the midday sun warmed the metal bleachers. This was the biggest game in school history, just as the past two in a row had been.

I listened intently on the outskirts of the kickoff return team's huddle as instructions were barked about setting the tone, sticking to blocks and winning this first fight. What I'd give to be in that huddle.

"McCann, are you there?" I heard Coach Perkins voice cracking over the two-way handheld radio in my pocket.

"Yes, sir! Loud and clear Coach Perk. Let's get it!" I said with genuine enthusiasm.

"Yes, sir," he said in his calm, even tone. "Keep the radio near you, I'm gonna need your eyes and ears down there on the sideline. I'm gonna miss having you on the field next year like this, it's been nice to have an inside scoop with the secondary."

"I got ya Coach!" If I couldn't be on the field I was determined to help us win somehow. Today, my job was to be an extra coach from the sideline while Coach Perkins viewed the game from the fourth floor of the stadium center.

Across the field, the metal bleachers on the eastern visitor's side of the field were packed with Chanticleer fans who made the two-hour journey from Conway, South Carolina. Their heads moved north to south in an arcing motion as they watched their first kickoff sail through the endzone underneath the scoreboard. Nearly 3,800 people, by far our largest home audience, made the atmosphere surreal. Our home field advantage had somehow slipped from our fingertips; this game was exciting!

Collin orchestrated a flawless start to the game, going four for four and capping the 80-yard drive with a 21-yard pass to our increasingly important transfer, Drew Rucks. Coastal started off slower offensively, only picking up a field goal on their first drive. We knew their sluggish pace wouldn't last for long though.

The Chanticleers possessed a number of offensive weapons,

some of whom were rumored to be NFL material, that we knew could hurt us if we didn't contain them. Quarterback Tyler Thigpen was at the center of the action. He had a cannon for an arm and he could move if he was flushed out of the pocket. Behind him were three reliable tailbacks. Aundres Perkins and Mike Tolbert, who looked more like defensive ends, and Patrick Hall, who was the lightning to their thunder. They had a strong offensive line who could give Thigpen time to throw and the running backs room to run, but the perimeter was hard to account for. Jerome Simpson, their answer to Maurice Price, stood 6'2", ran a 4:47 forty, and had massive hands. He didn't have terribly impressive numbers, but he was dangerous with the ball in his mitts. He was the team's playmaker and we knew they'd come to him when the game got tight.

Collin and the offense eagerly took the field for the second time to face the Chanticleer defense. The pre-game jitters were gone and we were ready to get back to work. The Coastal defense was anchored by their two top players, middle linebacker Maurice Simpkins and free safety Quinton Teal. Both could fly and they ob-

Maurice Simpkins (33) watches the Buccaneer offensive line for signs of movement. His talented defense is determined not to let Andre "Dre" Copeland (28) and the offense into the endzone.

viously possessed a sixth sense for finding the football, we knew that much from film.

We traded punts until Coastal assembled a hard fought 85-yard drive in which Thigpen and Hall carried their team down the field in 15 plays. We couldn't match their late half success and settled for a punt as the game clock ticked under one minute in the half. As we started the long hike toward the locker room for halftime I looked south at the scoreboard, 10-7 Chanticleers.

Coastal played a dominant half, but our shiny blue scoreboard didn't reflect it. We earned first downs or stops when we needed to, but we couldn't seem to make any big plays or find those breaks that had come to us in previous games. They forced us to grind for every yard on offense and seemed to constantly advance on our defense. In short, they were an above average team and we had to fight for every inch.

Nobody panicked. Helmets didn't fly. Nobody yelled or screamed, other than Coach Kelly, who always yelled and screamed. But even he seemed cooler than usual. I grabbed a few towels for my fellow DB's who were waiting in the back corner of the locker room as I walked past Toby and the athletic training staff at the threshold of the double doors.

We had no reason to worry, the game was well within our grasp. Offensively we had some drops and some missed opportunities. Defensively we needed to play their receivers tighter and wrap up sooner – "No more YAC!" as Coach Perkins had blared through the two-way in the second quarter.

Okeba and Jada were engaged in a passionate debate about a check to our "Black" coverage and whose responsibility the slant was when I arrived.

"In Black I play deep half, Jada," Okeba pleaded. "I can't get to that slant, *and* cover deep, you gotta help."

"I'm covering underneath and I gotta stop the run," said Jada in response, "they're getting a push every time."

Both Jada and Okeba were smart football players, and to some extent they were both right. Coastal was picking on a chink on our armor. Great tacticians exploit weaknesses they find, something Coach Mills and Collin understood well. Though it wasn't as much fun to watch it happen to us.

"Keeb, you're playing good," I reinforced Okeba's play, he was doing the right thing. "Gotta close faster on those deep passes, they're gonna try to get to Simpson." I passed out the hand towels along with a piece of advice for each of the starters as I went down the line. "CJ, you're playing good, gotta help them finish off those running backs. Tavares, you too. Mish, Jon, Marvin, the corners are playing good, they don't seem to be wanting to attack you guys outside much. Be ready, it's coming, don't get lulled to sleep."

Excitement was written all over their faces and adrenaline pumped through their veins. They had fire in their eyes and confidence in their hearts. Nothing could stop us, it didn't matter if we

Jay Mills (visor) had strategic reasons for every decision he made, including whether to kick extra points or attempt two-point conversions. Backup quarterbacks Eli Byrd (10) and Sidney Bryant (15) remained close to Mills throughout games to take notes and chart statistics.

were down by a field goal. We had them right where we wanted them. We didn't have to say much, we knew what was ahead of us. We knew what we had to do to win this game and it didn't involve much talking.

Coach Perkins spoke to the DB's, Coach Barrows pulled the defense together, and Coach Mills closed out halftime. Each man spoke about finishing. Finishing plays, finishing routes, finishing the game. Mills even dared to say finishing what we started for Eddie.

"One! Two! Champs!"

The choir of bass voices breaking down sounded fierce as sweaty bodies funneled toward the double doors of the locker room. Like cows being herded through a corral, we squeezed through the short hallway toward the afternoon sunlight. I took in one last whiff of locker room stench and looked above the blue double doors leading to the field. To myself I read the banner taped to the wall, "Every Man, Every Play, Every Day."

CHAPTER 31

DOORMAT

SATURDAY, NOVEMBER 19, 2005

NORTH CHARLESTON, SC

The third quarter was filled with sloppy offensive play and solid defense from both teams. Neither team dominated, but Coastal managed to slap together a touchdown drive to give themselves a 10- point lead. Hardly a crushing blow, but it still stung. We had come from behind before, 10 points was nothing.

As the fourth quarter came into view, our opportunities to put points on the board became fewer and fewer. Coastal was closing in on another score after Hall scampered to the edge of our red zone, 20 yards from paydirt.

"Let's go! Pick it up! Bend but don't break!" I could feel my voice getting hoarse, I hadn't stopped yelling all day. "Come on fellas, let's tighten up here!"

The bodies on the field remained unresponsive. They were tired, but not exhausted. CJ had his hands on his hips as his blue eyes carefully studied Coach Barrows' hands for the signal. Okeba stared, open-mouthed as he tried to suck up as much air as his lungs would allow. David Misher and Degraf were the only two on the field who acknowledged the cheers from the sideline with nods and a few claps of their own.

If we gave away another touchdown here, we'd be down by three scores. Not an impossible comeback, but not something we wanted to attempt, either. As the defense lined up I could see sweat beading off bodies and out of facemasks. Coastal looked winded but we didn't look much better. The Band of Brothers, Jada, Jonna, and Josh, lined up perfectly across the field in my line of vision. They had made dozens of plays today and we needed them now, Coastal was hammering their ground game to chew up as much clock as possible. The Chanticleers didn't need long runs or deep throws, they needed short first downs to keep the clock ticking. Patrick Hall exited the field and nobody was surprised when he was replaced with the larger back, Mike Tolbert.

Jada, Jonna, and Josh had become a trio to be reckoned with. Jada averaged more than 10 tackles per game. Josh was as mean as a viper and loved contact, smashing into linemen and backs at every opportunity. And Jonna had been dubbed the Big South Freshman of the Year a few years back when he amassed over 100 tackles during his first semester at college.

First down and 10. The Chanticleers lined up in a doubles formation with two receivers on either side of the offensive line. Only Thigpen and Tolbert were set five yards deep in the backfield.

Like the Red Sea, bodies parted left and right for the play to unfold in slow motion. Tolbert was set to receive the handoff as the offensive linemen took steps to their right side of the line of scrimmage. Zone blocking. Here comes the Zone Read. Tolbert stood 5'11" and was nearly as thick as he was tall, weighing close to 250 pounds. He wasn't going around anyone, the linebackers in front of me knew that at least one of them was in for a collision.

The Zone Read is a slow-developing play that allows the tailback to take his time while the linemen create holes with their zone-blocking technique. Tolbert ran at a slight angle toward the sideline with his shoulders almost perpendicular to the line of scrimmage as he scanned for a hole. In a flash, he saw his opportunity and made the cut upfield. His right foot dug into the torn up ground and his shoulders squared up with one smooth motion. The Tolbert Train was heading southbound toward the endzone.

Our trio of gladiators playing linebacker were the most capable group of putting a stop to this ground attack. The defensive line was being blocked and none of the DB's could stop Tolbert without him picking up the first down. Right now, the linebackers were our only hope. Josh was too far away to make a play on the far side of the field. Jada was being mauled by two Chanticleers and couldn't slip free. Jonna saw the sea of white Coastal jerseys part and Tolbert's stout frame pick up speed.

Jonna Lee stood 5'11" and was listed at 232 pounds. In reality, he weighed 250 pounds, 200 of which was in his butt and massive legs. In the previous spring he was the second strongest player on the squad, setting the team record with a 600-pound squat. Jonna's body language tightened when he saw Tolbert square up to him from 10 yards away.

The linebacker's shoulders were already square and his body had a forward lean so steep he would have fallen over if he wasn't in an all out sprint. Every one of us held our breath, our front row seats were about to get exciting. If Tolbert broke past Jonna, he had a clear shot to the endzone 20 yards away. The thick tailback approached the line of scrimmage and lowered his left shoulder, doing his best to lean into the impending strike from Jonna.

In the split-second before a full speed encounter, each person has the opportunity to back out. It's a chance to lighten your step and brace yourself for the pain you're about to put your body through. Your mind tells you it will hurt less if you just slow down. It's counterintuitive to think that the safest thing you can do is throw every ounce of your being into this other mass with all your might, but that's exactly what you have to do. The man that slows down is the man that loses. And if neither slows down, the fans are in for a show.

Like two trains on the same track steaming toward each other, nothing could prevent the inevitable carnage. 500 pounds of muscle collided at full speed. The facemasks made first contact, their bodies seemed to flatten out like a baseball being crushed by a bat in slow motion. Jonna's writhing arms and bare hands shot up from his sides to wrap around the back in case Tolbert tried to squirm. Both players legs kept moving and their bodies seemed to meld into one ball of explosive power. Grass was being pulled from the ground by Jonna's cleats and sweat flew from the bodies of both men. Tolbert's head snapped backwards and his legs lifted off the ground as Jonna's momentum took over the collision. The velocity of the linebacker was unmatched and Jonna took "Thunder" to the ground like a rag doll behind the line of scrimmage.

Like Romans watching a battle in the Colosseum, the stands echoed with cries of hysteria.

Jonna shot up from the tackle as he roared at the sky with clenched fists. Coastal was further back than when they started the play. Second down and 11. Momentum trickled all the way to the sideline and we celebrated the annihilation we had just witnessed. We were not ready to give up, the game was not over.

On the next play, a holding penalty pushed them 21 yards back from the first down marker just before Thigpen picked up a 16-yard scramble on third down. Fourth and five.

If they made the field goal attempt they were lining up for, we would only be down by two touchdowns with an entire quarter left to play. The score would only be 20-7 if they make this chip shot and it would give us plenty of time to do what we do best, score in a hurry. We had pulled out crazier wins than this. We played our best football under pressure.

The ball was snapped from our 15-yard line back to the holder for Coastal.

THUD

A single thud signaling connection echoed across the field to the sideline as the ball sailed upward. Up from the holder's hands. Up past the kicker's eyes. Up toward the goal posts. Another thud blasted from the scrum of bodies.

THUD

"Blocked!" I shouted. "Marvin blocked it off the edge!"

Bodies came screaming from the field with elation and adrenaline as we high fived and congratulated each one for a job well done. Two touchdowns would win the game for us. A touchdown and a field goal would tie it for us.

"Men," Coach Barrows choked out of his hoarse throat, "what have we been talking about since Gardner Webb? Huh? Believe! You gotta believe! Great job, great job! Now get some fluids and get some rest, we're gonna have to do it again as soon as the offense scores."

Heads nodded and the celebrations dried up as quick as they came. The defense needed to conserve their energy. Too much confidence brought mistakes. They smiled and chatted about adjustments, but we all knew the elation was temporary. We entered the fourth quarter down by 10 points, 17-7. Every 5:30 a.m. workout, every gasser during camp, every full padded practice, all of it lead to this point.

Momentum was on our side and our enthusiasm was rising with every play the offense shoved down Coastal's throat. First down, power right side. Dre broke a tackle in the backfield then put a move on the safety, Teal, that left the defender on his knees grabbing at air. 25 yards to end the third quarter.

Fourth quarter: eight-yard cut by Dre. Four-yard rush by Bobby. 18-yard pass to Murry! From the defensive bench we

Andre "Dre" Copeland (28) wasn't a big player, but his moves
and his explosive, compact running style made him hard to bring
down. Bryan Meers (11) hustles downfield in search of someone to block.

mocked the doormat line from the papers as we reminded each
other who had been expected to win.

His number had been called, but he didn't want to take the
field; he wanted us to score a touchdown instead. We weren't upset
with a field goal, but it wasn't a touchdown. None the less, we were
three points closer after Nick nailed a 22 yarder. 17-10 with just
under 10:00 to play.

Coach Barrows left the defense with one word as they took
the field, "Believe!" Five minutes later we had the ball back in our
hands on our own 39-yard line, ready to take the lead for the first
time this half.

Nick Ellis already made his field goal and we held up our end
of the bargain on defense. But the offense ran into some trouble.
The pick Collin just threw was going to make it immensely difficult for us to score that last touchdown. An, "I just blew it," look

was written all over his face as he and Coach Mills engaged in heated dialogue about what had just happened.

We had been here before. The situation was eerily similar to the season opener against The Citadel: big time stage, close game, down by a touchdown, interception. The last time this happened we couldn't compose ourselves and The Citadel scored three unanswered touchdowns.

Coastal took over with 3:38 left on the clock. If we held them, we would have one more opportunity to score that final touchdown we needed. No additional motivation was necessary from the coaches when the defense took the field. One series is all we had. One series to get the ball back. One series to win a championship. One series to define this roller coaster season.

Jada started off the series with a five-yard tackle for loss. That's one. My roommates, Josh and CJ, combined for the next tackle after Hall managed to gain two yards. That's two. Thigpen made a scramble but was caught by Jada and Degraf as the clock ticked

CJ Hirschman (22) tackles Coastal Carolina quarterback Tyler Thigpen (16) while Josh Mitchell (51) and Stonewall Randolph III (standing) assist.

under 3:00 to play. That's three.

We anxiously watched the Chanticleer sideline to see if head coach Dave Bennett was crazy enough to go for it on fourth down. He looked confident. He took off his black hat and rubbed his head with his hand, as if to check if he'd lost some hair from the stress of the game. When he replaced the hat his eyes narrowed and his mustached upper lip drew tight. He barked an order and encouraged the punt team with a few forceful claps as he waved them onto the field. Obviously not what he wanted to do. Offensive linemen moaned and skill players threw their hands in the air as their punt team replaced the offense.

After the punt, we'd have to go down and score another touch-down to tie it up. The punt team lined up for action. Maybe Coach Mills would go for two again like we did against VMI. Maybe he'd kick the extra point this time and take it into overtime. The long snapper tightened his grip on the ball and whipped it between his legs.

To Markus Murry, who stood with his heels on the 10-yard line, Aundres Perkins looked like a small offensive lineman with the ball tucked under his left arm. Perkins' number one jersey squeezed his bustling 6'2" frame as he cut around the corner of the punt team and steamed toward the Buccaneer sideline. Tavares should have been back there, not up trying to block this punt, Markus was just the backup. Tavares was more experienced, he would have made sense of all that chatter before the play, he would have a better chance of saving the game. Perkins' footsteps felt like an earthquake growing louder and louder as Markus sprinted the sideline, no clue how he was going to slow him down.

Like a man trying to tackle a truck, Perkins steamrolled Markus without so much as a hitch. As he rolled over on his back, Markus could see Perkins' heels cross into the endzone. Perkins 46-yard fake punt rush put Coastal Carolina up by two touchdowns with 2:50 left in the championship game.

The sinking of our hearts reverberated louder than Coastal's cheers about getting to the playoffs. They looked to each other and pointed at their ring fingers. We looked aimlessly with palms facing upwards, stunned. They delighted in the fact that they had just pulled the rug out from under us, stretching their lead back out to two touchdowns. We moped around the sidelines, speechless.

We were *supposed* to win this game. We were *supposed* to honor the Gadson family with our season. We were not *supposed* to be the doormat of the Big South.

CHAPTER 32

GOING DOWN SWINGING

SATURDAY, NOVEMBER 19, 2005

NORTH CHARLESTON, SC

The sideline remained silent as we picked up the pieces of our broken hearts. Though many of the fans had begun to shuffle out of the stadium, there was still some football to muscle through. Our hopes and dreams had been shattered, but it wasn't time to take off our pads and call it a season. Not yet, at least. The game clock read 2:49 after we brought the ball to the 21-yard line on the ensuing kickoff.

Collin Drafts had always been a default leader for the team. He played a position that required leadership and he had become the face of our program. CSU even had life-size cardboard cutouts of him made for promotional events. He encouraged teammates and corrected players when they missed assignments, but he had never been the vocal leader who gives a speech and fires up the team's engine. We knew we could count on his legs and his arm, but he'd never stepped into the role of team motivator. Until now. I could hear him encouraging the offense like never before as they took the field. He didn't seem phased by what had just happened. His demeanor reflected a confident attitude, he had been here before. He just kept repeating, "One play at a time."

Body language tells all. Unfortunately, most everyone in a blue jersey looked defeated.

"Trey Right, Reno, Big Ben, Orlando," Collin snapped at the offense. A sprint out to the right, the play was designed to go to Markus on a 20-yard out route. The sprint out afforded him time to scan the field. Collin must have known something the rest of us didn't. Somehow he spotted a different receiver sneaking past the safety. Drew Rucks wasn't supposed to be the target, but he was 50 yards downfield and it was worth a throw. Why not? We had nothing to lose, anyway. As we looked downfield we saw Rucks passing the safety and start to stumble. Oh no, Collin overthrew him. He's falling. He caught it! Drew ended up on Coastal's 15-yard line, scoring position. We Believe.

Pleading with his defense to make a play or for the refs to throw a flag in their favor, Dave Bennett fell to his knees on the

After throwing an interception earlier in the fourth quarter, Collin Drafts (7) calmed down and led the team with the authority of a five star general.

opposing sideline. A slant, couple of penalties in our favor, and a blind scramble through traffic by Collin put us back in the ball game, 24-16. With hope in their voices, the offense came back to the sideline repeating, "That's one, let's do it again!"

"They're not dead, yet!" rang over the loudspeakers of the stadium. Although terribly inappropriate, given the huge black dot on the grass before us, we loved the sound of it.

Nick lined up for the extra point to bring us within seven of the Chanticleers.

THUD-THUD

"Oh no…" I said under my breath. "They blocked it. Please tell me that flag is on them."

"Offside, on the defense," said the referee in the white hat. "Half the distance to the goal. Re-kick."

Attempt two sailed through with ease. 24-17, Chanticleers.

My bones ached to be on the field and be in the action but I was trapped on the sideline. Not much chatter buzzed on the two-way since the fake punt. Maybe the coaches were headed down to the sideline to congratulate us on our first winning season and a hard-fought game. I found the nearest marker board and scribbled "B-E-L-I-E-V-E" on it with "EG21" in both corners in black ink. I showed the whittled crowd the marker board and reminded them what we were playing for. I ran up and down the sideline shouting, "We buh-lieve! We buh-lieve!" as our onside kick team set up to get the ball back for us. If we recovered the onside kick, we'd have a shot at scoring one more time and taking the game to overtime. We came so close to beating Coastal in 2004 and we had come so far this year, we would never give up hope. If Eddie was on the sideline he wouldn't let us give up. We made a promise to his family and to each other that we would play to the very end. That we would win a conference championship to honor him.

Coaches often talk about learning to win; up until a few weeks ago I had no clue what they were babbling about. You play hard and you win, you don't play hard and you lose. But it hit me like an Oklahoma drill. It hit all of us. It takes focus to close a game out. It takes concentration to keep your assignments for all four quarters and not get distracted. Without all that experience during close games from 2004 and earlier this year, we would never know how to close out these types of games. But we had learned the hard way, and we were prepared to do it again. We did it against Gardner Webb. We did it against Liberty. And we were ready to do it right now, we just had to get the ball back.

The whole team knelt and joined hands on the sideline facing the onside kick team. The kickoff team setup with five players on the far side of the field and six players lined up near us. Nick aimed the tee toward our sideline. This wasn't going to be a surprise, everyone knew where the ball was headed.

The six nearside players got down into sprinter's stances and eyed up the men 10 yards away. Assignments were simple: Priority number one was the ball. If you had a chance, go for it. If you couldn't get the ball, hit somebody. Like bulls stamping their hooves in rage, the kickoff team dug their cleats into the grass to get a good starting position. We believe.

Nick Ellis toed the gut of the football into the torn-up grass as the "Hit Squad," as deemed by Coach Perkins, bolted for their marks. One small hop. Big second hop! Blue helmets with cutlasses and black helmets with roosters soared as the ball came down from its high bounce. Right into the hands of their biggest playmaker, Jerome Simpson. 1:39 on the clock. Coastal just received a fresh set of downs to finish the game. Reality set in, again. Today was not our day.

The remaining fans, now less than 1,000, again began to straggle out of the stadium. Coastal would run the clock out and win the game. The fans had seen enough heartache for one day. We played a hard fought game. They couldn't bear to see the trophy ceremony. The commissioner himself was already pacing the Coastal sideline, ready to give Dave Bennett's hand a congratulatory shake.

Some would call it fate, others astute coaching. Either way, Coach Mills had been frugal with our timeouts. He had three left to burn. As the Chanticleer offense jogged onto the field, every person on our half of the stadium was doing the math in their head. If we could stop them in four downs, using all those timeouts, we would have one more shot at getting the ball back. It may only be a few seconds, but that's better than nothing. One chance was all the hope we needed. We hadn't come this far to unravel because of a little pressure.

LET'S GO BUCS! LET'S GO BUCS! LET'S GO BUCS!

First and 10. 1:38 on the clock. Coastal lined up in the "Victory" formation and took a knee. Timeout, our last of the game. Second and 11. Victory formation. Thigpen meandered in the pocket until it was collapsed by CJ and Okeba off the edges. Tick, tick, tick. Third and 17. The clock ticked to 49 seconds. Victory formation. Thigpen protected the ball with both hands as carefully as a newborn and took another knee. Tick. Tick. Tick. Their strategy was working. 10 seconds on the game clock.

The sideline judge's whistle tooted for a timeout from Dave Bennett. Eyes studied the Coastal sideline more closely than any test we'd ever encountered. We knew they were going to drain the clock. They would probably line up in a punt formation and have someone scramble out of the back of the endzone, giving us two points and a loss. We had practiced the play dozens of times during Coach Mills' "special situations" segments. Everyone on our sideline knew what Coastal had to do. Our defense, still throbbing with adrenaline from the last three plays, knew what they had to do to stop them. Get the man with the ball tackled before he gets to the endzone. If he gets to the endzone, get him out as soon as possible so we can have an opportunity to return the kick.

Our last chance to stay in the game. Their last chance to put us away. The entire season came down to this play – again. Every ounce of sweat in the offseason. Every tear we shed for Eddie. Every grueling workout we put ourselves through. Our backs had been pressed against the wall for three weeks straight. We had applied unimaginable pressure on ourselves. More film. Extra reps. Less distractions. Every win we fought for came down to this play.

The remaining fans, now numbered in the low hundreds instead of the thousands, pressed against the chain link fence. Like us, they still believed.

I saw my dismissed teammates wearing street clothes accented with regret and the same tortured look I sported from the sideline. I saw family, mine and others, all gathered on the chain link fence that overlooked the track at the base of the bleachers. In the middle of the crowd of parents stood a tall black man with a white hat and matching white shirt that read "Edward A. Gadson" arched over the top. Mr. Gadson, accompanied by his best friend Mitch, had walked down out of his seat to get a closer look at how this would play out. He wondered if this would be the fairy tale ending of a season or if this would just be a nice try. Mrs. Gadson watched from Mitch's home a few miles up the road with his wife, Peggy.

I became antsy and grabbed the marker board again. "We buh-lieve! We buh-lieve! We buh-lieve!" The meager crowd joined me and the chant continued even after I directed my attention back to the field.

Jerome Simpson, the receiver we had been so concerned about, lined up as the "punter." His job was not to punt, rather to avoid being tackled and run the remaining 10 seconds from the clock. Specialty plays, such as this, are only used once every few years. They are delicate and, if needed, potentially game-changing. Simpson and the Chanticleers had never practiced this special formation. Ever.

The ball spiraled back to Simpson's hands and he sprinted backwards, away from the defense, toward his own endzone. Okeba came unblocked, barreling off of the offense's left side to try and pin Simpson between the hashmark and the numbers near the 10-yard line. He forced Simpson into a corner as he recalled his basketball days, shadowing Simpson's every move and keeping his own body in front of Simpson. All of a sudden, Simpson planted his left foot and darted toward the orange pylon at the corner of the South endzone.

CJ shot off the opposite side of the offensive line before being blatantly held. CJ momentarily threw his hands up in the air looking for a penalty flag from the sideline judge. He quickly realized the sideline judge wasn't paying attention and he wasn't getting a flag. He spun out of the hold and tossed his blocker to the ground, locking eyes on Simpson. No blockers stood in his way and he closed the gap on Simpson right as Okeba was forcing him to the corner of the endzone. If he gave it everything, he might be able to get there.

The crowd's noise built to a crescendo and we simultaneously saw the same thing as CJ. Instead of heading out of the endzone, Simpson peeled toward the corner of the field. CJ had gotten close enough to hear Simpson laughing and taunting his way back to the five-yard marker. CJ had one chance to get the ball back and nobody was close enough to help, he had to punch it out. His body was exhausted and he should probably be in a sling on the sideline with this dang shoulder, but he was the only person who could get to the corner in time. He couldn't quite get his hands on Simpson, but managed to spin him out of bounds at the three yard line. He punched at the ball with everything his body would give. But he whiffed.

Bennett took off his hat and pointed South. He disapprovingly shouted, "Out of the endzone!" Too little, too late. With one swift motion, every eyeball in the stadium turned to the game clock on our shiny new scoreboard. The clock read 01:5. We believe!

The turmoil of the previous play spilled onto the sideline as the defense came sprinting toward us shouting, "Finish! Finish!" in the direction of the offense. They couldn't hear, they were too focused on Coach Mills. He demanded every sliver of their attention. "Reno Bingo" was the call. A spinoff play from the one used to beat VMI back in 2004. Offense ran this play so many times it had become as familiar to them as their own mouthpieces. Mills broke the huddle with a clap that could be heard in the parking lot where cars were lined up to leave campus.

Every muscle in my body tensed up. This was it. This was why we watched film for hours on end. This was why we got up early to meet before class. This was why we opted for a different college experience. All for the opportunity to be on this field at this moment.

The offense lined up unbalanced with the tight end, Bryan Meers, on the left side of the line of scrimmage. Outside of him the tackle, Troy James, lined up as the bookend. Collin called the shift, opening Meers for eligibility as Troy James hustled to the right side of the line of scrimmage for added protection. In his mind, Collin would roll right, simulating the exact play from the year prior. The defense would flow to Meers on the opposite side of the field while Dre would be open shallow in the flats, just a few yards from Collin.

But NFL teams were scouting Maurice Simpkins. "Tight end's eligible! Tight end's eligible! Watch for a trick play the other way!" he screamed through his mouthpiece, locking eyes on our quarterback as if to say, "Not today, Drafts."

Collin's movements hastened as he watched Simpkins communicate the play to his teammates. He would have to make something happen quickly. He'd been doing it all season, improvising his way into touchdowns and wins. He had a knack for the pressure and he performed best when this sort of danger was impending. Collin had become a great quarterback because he was willing to take necessary risks. But they were just that, risks. The outcomes weren't guaranteed and his streak was bound to end at some point. On the field he didn't take stupid risks. They were calculated risks that a less experienced player wouldn't have made. He made aggressive decisions and he knew when his back was against the wall he had to force something to happen.

This gadget play was designed to test Coastal mentally and give us the upper hand through confusion. They weren't confused and we didn't have the upper hand when Dre crept in motion behind the offensive line, toward the hopefully-open-flats. The ball flung back between Huntsinger's legs and Collin sprinted right, away from the tight end who everyone in the stadium now knew was eligible. The offensive line, which had been playing a tough game all day, seemed to crumble on either side and both defensive ends simultaneously broke from their would be blockers to tackle our last hope.

Collin bolted through his reads. First read, Dre: covered. Second read, Rucks: covered. Backside to Price: covered. Collin pulled up his sprint as he saw the defender in front of him and sensed the other behind. The shot was risky, but it was his only choice.

Off of his back foot, Collin slung a pass across his body and over the head of the first defensive end who had already wrapped his arms around Collin's trunk and had begun taking him to the ground. The ball floated over Rick Howell and Shawn Huntsinger's heads while they blocked their men, no idea that our last hope was soaring inches from their helmets. The ball wobbled past the right outstretched arm of Maurice Simpkins as he recognized what was happening a split-second too late. Two Coastal players closed in on the ball as it crossed the goal line and headed toward someone in blue. Someone who should have been making a pick for Dre. Someone who was completely out of position, but somehow open. Someone who had already stepped up to fill a big pair of shoes. If he dropped it, nobody would blame him, it was a tough ball to catch and he wasn't a tenured veteran. The ball screeched to a halt in a navy blue belly as its owner was sandwiched by two Coastal defenders.

"Caught! Caught! Caught! Markus Murry! Markus

Murry with the touchdown!" screamed the announcer. "24-23, no time on the clock. Holy cow! Somebody's watching out for the Buccaneers!"

Mouths hung open on the Chanticleer sideline and Bennett dropped his head. "They might go for two!" was all he could muster.

The couple hundred people left in the stands sounded like 50,000 strong. We couldn't contain ourselves. We jumped and screamed and gripped each other's jerseys. Did that really happen? Collin couldn't see anything from underneath the defensive linemen but he knew something great had happened from the crowd's reaction. Murry popped up as quickly as he had been knocked down, scrambling to find someone to celebrate with.

We high fived and hugged every man who came spilling off the field. Somehow the coaches remembered to bring us back to reality. We were still down by one point, the game had not been won. Coach Mills had yet to signal for a two-point conversion or a kick.

CHAPTER 33

BELIEVE

SATURDAY, NOVEMBER 19, 2005

NORTH CHARLESTON, SC

Not a snowball's chance in Charleston was Nick Ellis going to miss that extra point. Not with this opportunity, not today. In mere seconds the game was tied 24-24. We were headed to overtime. We Believe!

An out-of-place calm swept over the sideline as our captains, Degraf, Meers, and the offensive linemen Harrison and Huntsinger walked to midfield to meet our opponents. While the referees explained that overtime rules allow for each team to get one possession before that overtime period ends, Coach Mills gathered the offense to talk about their first plays. Degraf deferred the ball to give Coastal the first scoring opportunity on offense. As soon as he saw the signal, Coach Barrows gathered the defense to glaze over strategy before giving us a few words of encouragement.

The ball was placed at the 25-yard line of the south endzone, facing the scoreboard. We broke the huddle on "Champs!" and the starting defense trotted onto the field. Excitement, tension, anticipation, and nervousness all ran through our veins faster than any drug ever could.

I turned the opposite direction to make sure the crowd knew how important this was. The marker board shot up in the air and the chant began again, "We buh-lieve! We buh-lieve! We buh-lieve!" By now they had caught on and a chorus of fans shouted at the top of their lungs with smiles on their faces and fists in the sky. People had abandoned their cars in the parking lot and were pressed against the chain link fence overlooking our sideline. Not a single person sat in the bleachers as Coastal's offense took the field for their first drive.

The Coastal Carolina offensive line settled their heavy feet into formation just yards away from the large black dot that read "EG21" in the center. They marched to the line of scrimmage in a business-like, no nonsense manner. They had been loose all game, but attitudes shifted and they concentrated on their objective. For the first time since the first quarter, they were on their heels.

The first play, a run, went to Patrick Hall on the left side of the offensive line. Jada almost made the tackle in the backfield, but "Lightning" cut for seven yards before being brought down. The threat became real, we couldn't give up that kind of real estate and come out ahead. Second down was better, only three yards, but we gave up a new set of downs. First and 10 for the Chants as our defendable territory continued to shrink. First down: zone read left. Second down: power up the middle. Third down: sprint out to their right!

Thigpen, whose cannon of an arm could thread most needles, took off looking for a deep out route near the goal line. Mish saw the whole play unfold and batted the ball down with his right hand as he kept his left on the hip of the receiver and simultaneously drug him to the ground. Perfect execution on a huge third down. Fourth down brought the field goal team and the first score of overtime: 27-24, Chanticleers.

Collin and the offense started in the same position as Thigpen and his crew, the 25 yard line facing the scoreboard. The game clock still read 0:00 as the play clock began its countdown from 25. Dre stumbled for a few yards before Price and Drew Rucks each dropped a pass. Fourth down came sooner than expected.

"Come on man, you gotta do this for us!" Nick just looked at me and smiled his, aw shucks smile as he looked at his feet. He didn't need to say anything, he gave me a nod and hustled to get lined up for his 41 yard field goal attempt.

Nick lined up with the wind at his back and his eyes on Marvin McHellon's hands in the dirt. Back three steps, always stepping back with his left foot first, then left two steps. Nick cocked his body toward Marvin and aimed his right foot at Marvin's marked spot. His mind had to be racing about the pressure of the situation. How close victory was for us. How much this meant to us and to Eddie's dad in the front row pressed against the chain link fence. The snap was high, but Marvin pulled it down in time to bring it to the perfect spot and put the slightest angle on it. No time to think, just do his job. "Ice in his veins" is how Dad would have described Nick. He didn't get nervous, he just kicked field goals. Seconds later the ball split the uprights. The kick would have gone through from 51 yards.

Our faces hurt from smiling and our throats were sore from screaming. This was more fun than any party could ever be.

Nick wasn't looking for praise, although he was showered with it as he jogged back to the sideline. He just wanted to win like the rest of us. Before he took his place on the sideline, he did his best Eddie Gadson grin, tapped his chest with open palms, and rubbed his forefingers together with his thumbs to let us know he was "money." We believe!

Coach Kelly, who typically reserved his words for the offensive line, shouted out something about not being anyone's doormat as the field goal unit hustled back to the sideline. I gave a few pumps of the marker board and encouraged the already ecstatic crowd to join us in the brief celebration.

The blue scoreboard read 27-27. Coastal's defense huddled on the field near their sideline, mirroring our offense. The same units would return in two minutes to attempt their same respective goals, this was our turn to take the lead on offense. We would set the pace for the second overtime period and Coastal would have to match the points, if any, we put on the board.

The day had become gray and dreary, like our fairy tale could be rained on at any moment. There were no lights for the late afternoon play, our modest crowds could never justify the investment. The stadium didn't thunder with applause. Instead, a couple hundred people chanted "We believe!" from the other side of the chain link fence. None of that mattered, the atmosphere didn't reflect our attitude.

BEEEP

Nick Ellis (13) attempts the biggest kick of his career from 41 yards out with Marvin McHellon (26) holding for him. If Ellis makes the kick, the game goes into double overtime.

The offense lined back up on the 25-yard line looking worn, but determined. Collin and Coach Mills seemed to share a brain, reading each other's lips and finishing each other's sentences from halfway across the field.

We started strong on first and 10 as Dre gashed up the middle for four yards behind the tough blocking of the offensive line. Second down looked bleak as Collin sprinted out to his left, being chased down by a Coastal defender. He popped open his hips and squeezed a pass into Murry's arms right as the defender closed the gap and put Collin's facemask in the dirt. First down.

We rode Dre for another short gain before feeding Maurice Price a quick slant that turned into another first down. Coach Mills wanted to run the ball, we had pushed our luck to this point, no need for elaborate plays with the endzone so close. Dre lined up seven yards deep in the backfield with Jim O'Connor set as the fullback. I whispered Jim's name, knowing he'd gone the wrong way earlier in the game. This was his chance for redemption if Mills read off the fullback lead play from the playsheet tucked in his pants.

Jim took off left, followed by Dre. Jim got inside of Maurice Simpkins, the linebacker who seemed to make every other play on defense, and turn him out just enough. Dre squeezed through on a tough, inside run, dragging two defenders with him into the endzone. It was a play we wouldn't have been able to make the year prior. A play which we learned how to finish with only this season. The mini-celebration began again, knowing Coastal was about to have their turn. I read Jim's lips as he popped up from underneath the pile. He spewed something colorful, as only a guy from Jersey would come up with. Whatever it was, we could all agree. We took the lead for the first time since the second quarter. 34-27, Buccaneers.

WE BELIEVE! It was no longer a war cry we shouted across the field, it had become a statement. We no longer aimed our shouts across the field, we looked at each other as we enjoyed our brief celebration. We weren't trying to convince anyone, they could see it in our body language, in the fight we kept bringing to the field. We would never give up.

Coastal Carolina was poised to go to the playoffs for the first time in school history. Their 9-1 record indicated that they were an above-average football team who had already learned how to finish. They knew what they had to do to beat us. A field goal would not suffice, they needed to score a touchdown.

First and 10 for "all the marbles" I could hear one fan screaming in his South Carolina accent from across the track. Judging by their first play call, Tyler Thigpen and the Chanticleers offense were frustrated. They were tired of messing around with us. They wanted an end to this madness. Thigpen dropped back seven yards after a playaction fake to look for Jerome Simpson deep in the endzone. Marvin knew what was coming and positioned himself perfectly, cutting Simpson's route short with his body.

Second and 10 was supposed to be a gimme out in the flats near their sideline, but the running back couldn't wrangle in the wild pass. Third and 10 is when the pressure began to mount. The entire offense's body language tensed up and our fan section cheered just a notch louder. The Chants lined up in a passing formation, but only to distract us. Jonna wasn't fooled. He took one read step and he was on his way downhill to punish the ball carrier for a short gain.

Coastal used their only timeout of the overtime period to re-group. Black and white Chanticleer uniforms slumped as they took their time getting to the far sideline. They unbuckled their chinstraps and looked at the coaches approaching them on the edge of the field.

In contrast, Jonna, still frenzied from the last play's violence, lead the defense back to our sideline with an unmistakable bounce in his step. The rest of the defense followed suit, pumping fists and jogging back to our sideline with fire in their eyes. We joined them at the numbers, passing out high fives and "atta-boy's" to as many players as we could find. They needed to know they had support. They needed to know we believed in their ability to finish this game. Their mood was loose, we had nothing to lose. We weren't expected to win. We weren't expected to shock the world in double overtime. We had been "beat" two or three times now, this was nothing but a bonus.

Coach Barrows gave the defense some scenarios through his raspy, worn-out voice. He did his best to keep us grounded with his facial expressions but we knew how bad he wanted this, too. Across the field, Dave Bennett spoke with focus. His senior players repeated "Finish" over and over like a Southern Baptist congregation egging on their pastor.

Over our shoulders "One more play!" was being repeated by our parents and Eddie's dad, the only people left in the stadium. We couldn't see his face, but he was smiling. He had been ready to console us just moments ago. He had already walked down out of the stands prepared to tell us how hard we had worked, how proud of us he was, and how much our efforts meant to him and his family. He was prepared to tell us that it was okay we didn't win a championship for his son. But that was minutes ago, right now he was happy he didn't have to speak those words.

WE BUH-LIEVE! WE BUH-LIEVE! WE BUH-LIEVE!

Coastal lined up for fourth and six, a passing down. Almost 30 yards of field to defend, including our endzone, were spread in front of the defense. Coastal may run it, but chances were slim, our defensive line had been handling their business since halftime.

"G. Double Fire. Florida." I watched Coach Barrows curl his hand into a "G." Then he sprinkled his hands downward, like his fingers rained fire. Then he gave a Florida Gator "chomp" with both hands and gave a clap to signal that was his final answer.

"G Double Fire Florida! G Double Fire Florida!" I repeated. I sprinted through coverage responsibilities in my head as fast as I could, analyzing responsibilities and where our threats would be. G Double Fire Florida was a blitz, Barrows wanted finish this once and for all.

Coastal came out with two wide receivers on either side of the offensive line, a formation that called for a check into "Black" coverage. The blitz was off. We were now playing with two high safeties, CJ and Okeba. Thigpen and Hall awaited the snap in the shotgun formation. Okeba lined up on the defensive right's deep half and CJ on the defensive left, each lined up outside of the hash marks nearly 12 yards deep. Marvin and David would be underneath on the outside in case Coastal tried something short. Jada and Jonna had shallow route responsibilities, they should force Thigpen to throw it over their heads or outside of them. The defensive line setup with their ears pinned back like rabid dogs, ready to pounce at the first sign of movement.

The heavy feet of the offensive linemen took stomping steps backwards and their hands pulled into their chests, ready to punch. "Pass! Pass! Pass!"

Thigpen dropped back and eyed his target, planting his right foot and cocking his right arm for the far side of the field. My eyes flashed toward Okeba and Marvin to see if they were in position for the throw. Marvin faced us between his shallow man and the man arcing deep over his shoulder, perfect position. Okeba, who had deep half responsibilities, had already broken his back pedal and headed toward the line of scrimmage. Something was wrong. He must not have seen the corner route in the front tip of the endzone, Okeba was completely out of position.

CHAPTER 34

EG21

SATURDAY, NOVEMBER 19, 2005

NORTH CHARLESTON, SC

The crisp afternoon air was kicked around playfully by a light breeze. The autumn sun began to sink across the eastern tree line beyond the near-empty visitors' bleachers. Everyone in the stadium held their breath for the outcome of this fourth and six play.

Okeba had an instinctual reaction, something he felt in his gut, that told him they'd come back to this play. He recognized it from the second quarter. Jada chewed him out for not jumping the route, even though the slant wasn't *his* responsibility. Not again. This became an opportunity, this was his play. Okeba saw the man over his shoulder heading deep. He politely disregarded him, that wasn't their playmaker. He also saw Simpson on the slant, a route that would give Coastal a first down. He knew Thigpen would give his playmaker a chance for redemption. He would try to put the ball in Simpson's hands just like he had earlier in the game.

Okeba broke out of his backpedal without hesitation. The trajectory of his break cutoff Simpson's slant route. His big hands flashed up for the catch.

WE BUH-LIEVE! WE BUH-LIEVE! WE BUH-LIEVE!

When we let out our breathe for the first time in what seemed like hours, the ball was on the ground and the game was over. 34-27, Bucs win!

Okeba never broke stride. He sprinted parallel to the Chanticleer sideline scissoring his arms across his chest signaling "no-no" like a referee and waving at the Coastal sideline, telling them "bye bye" before throwing his helmet in the air. The field burst into a celebration like a Roman Candle being fired onto the field.

Dad, somewhere in the stands, shouted to my brother, "And that's why they play the game!"

Pandemonium broke out in Buccaneer field. Weeks, months of tension discharged as we poured from the sidelines to dog pile on Okeba. Gloves flew in the air and helmets were dropped on the sideline, nothing mattered except finding someone to celebrate with.

The fans were just behind us hopping the chain link fence and bounding onto the field across the red rubber track. Ed Gadson led the pack in his white shirt that read "Edward A. Gadson" on the front, nearly skipping across the field with elation. Within seconds every person behind the chain link fence had found a way onto the grass. The field had become a 120-yard party filled with players, family, and students all rejoicing with each other.

Everything around me blurred as I ran to hug Okeba and scream how proud I was into his ear. We hugged and I high fived him and slapped him in the chest with pride.

I ran through teammates and coaches alike, hugging and congratulating them with a joy I had never experienced. There were no words, only expressions and cheers. Bodies moved in every direction like anxious ants protecting the colony after being stepped on.

I was out of breath and my face hurt from the smile that had been stretched across my face. Out of the corner of my tear-filled eye, I saw a small group sprinting toward the southwest corner of the field where Eddie's black dot was painted on the grass. I dodged through the crowd of bodies to join a handful of teammates and we fell to the ground and hugged the black grass that read "EG21." We pounded the black spray painted earth and told Eddie that this was for him, this was his season, his championship.

"This is what Eddie wanted, man," Darius said through his South Carolina drawl and a few tears. "All he wanted was to win, he hated 'dem boys. And we did it for him!" With open palms we all slapped the black grass under us in agreement. "Even when things don't go the way you want, you can never give up. Never settle. You can never accept what others think is supposed to happen, you have to make your own path!"

On the far end of the field Coastal players trickled off, leaving

We gathered at Eddie's dot to celebrate with our brother.

breadcrumbs of tape, the occasional tear, and their playoff hopes behind them. A few of our remaining students carried out their duties as proud fans and vigorously climbed the goal posts, hanging and bouncing on the teetering ends. Though small in number, they were determined to bring it down. They eventually tore it down, ripped it out of the ground, and threw its remains into the pond by the locker room. The scene boosted our egos, it was something we could never have imagined.

One by one, as they finished congratulating Coastal on a hard fought game, players came to pay homage to Eddie with a hug of the dot and fist on the grass. Mr. Gadson had weaved his way through the crowd to his son's memorial, the black dot no longer visible from the stands beneath the congregation of blue jerseys and gold pants. He acted like one of us, hugging fiercely and refusing to hide an ounce of emotion. The team cocooned around him one last time and broke it down on "EG21" before Coach Mills called order to the chaos with a few cheerful spurts of his whistle.

In keeping with college football upset tradition, a meager crowd of fans was determined to bring down the goalposts. The goalposts were carried to the lake and eventually removed from campus by a mischievous trio of football players.

Mills ordered us down on a knee for our post-game ritual, a saying of the Lord's Prayer. Mom loved the sight of it, though we sped through the prayer significantly faster than she was used to hearing.

Our Father, who art in heaven,

hallowed be thy Name,

thy kingdom come,

thy will be done,

on earth as it is in heaven.

Give us this day our daily bread.

And forgive us our trespasses,

as we forgive those

who trespass against us.

And lead us not into temptation,

but deliver us from evil.

For thine is the kingdom,

and the power, and the glory,

for ever and ever. Amen.

Afterwards, Coach Mills delivered an uncharacteristically short postgame speech. "We had a guardian angel watching over us this fall down the stretch. He would be proud! I want to take this moment to hand out a game ball. One that, by the way, is going to say, 'Big South Conference Champions!'"

We roared with deafening howls of victory before Mills could finish his sentence. With the black "EG21" dot tattooed on his white sleeve, he thrust the ball high in the air. "Look what yard line it ended up on..."

Echoes of "twenty one" rang across the field as everyone

looked toward the center of the field. Fourth down and six from the CSU 21-yard line was the last play recorded in the championship game. The game ended on the exact yard marker with the big black dot that read "EG21" in the center.

"I'll make this brief, as I know you want to celebrate responsibly," Mills added. "But let me give this game ball out. It's the only one we're giving out today."

The game ball would only go to one person, an honor several players could have earned. CJ for pushing Simpson out of bounds. Collin for throwing two touchdowns and orchestrating the offense. Markus for catching the touchdown that sent us to overtime. Jada for the ridiculous 17 tackles he amassed. Okeba for the game-winning play. Nick for the 41-yarder he nailed in the first overtime. One person, above all, deserved the game ball.

"Game ball goes to Ed Gadson."

The crowd, which now included a couple hundred fans as

An emotional Ed Gadson holding his game ball high for the crowd to see.

well as the team, erupted with cheers. An immediate "Eddie! Eddie! Eddie!" chant started while Coach Mills embraced Ed Gadson with a strong, sincere hug.

Ed's all white t-shirt stuck out amongst the sea of blue jerseys. He stood in the center of us with his new leather gift held high in the air. His face was fragile. His mouth gave us congratulations and his arms gave every one of us hugs. But his eyes reminded us that today was still bitter-sweet. Ed Gadson wiped the tears from the corner of his eyes and began a clear, concise speech full of pride. "Guys, the last couple months you guys took it upon yourselves to dedicate the season to Eddie. And you told me you were going to bring the championship home. When the season started out, it was looking a little iffy." A low rumble of laughter and you-can-say-that-again glances made their way through the crowd. "You guys... you guys, stepped up. I was there with you every game, whether I was here in the stadium, on the golf course with the game on my cell phone, or at home listening to it on the internet. I was there with you every day. This means a heck of a lot to me and my family. CSU will always be number one in my heart."

It's unfair to say that a game can overcome death. A trophy could never be swapped for an individual, especially a person as unique as Eddie. But in some miniscule way, the 2005 Buccaneers helped provide healing for the Gadson family. Besides the few players with children, most of us could not yet fathom the love Ed and Paula Gadson have for their son. Through the adversity we faced and the determination we displayed, we were able to show the Gadsons what their son meant to us. The championship wasn't, as Ed Gadson called it, "just a win." We played for the win, but more importantly, we played for Eddie and the Gadson family. The greatest honors for loved ones are the stories of how their loss inspired others. Eddie Gadson inspired us all to believe.

The 2005 Charleston Southern Buccaneers,
Big South Conference Champions.

To view more images from the Coastal game, go to http://BelieveEG21.com/coastal

EPILOGUE

Saturday November 19, 2005 we received our Big South Conference Championship trophy. A trophy that still resides, unmatched by another, in the Buccaneer field house. After the spring game the following semester, a white championship banner with gold trim was hung from the ceiling of the Buc Dome with the other sports' championship banners. "2005" was stitched into the top left corner, signaling the first championship in school history.

Our championship rings were presented to us as the banner was unveiled. The record books will always label us as "Co-Champions" with Coastal due to the lack of tie-breaker verbiage in the rule books. But encircling the sapphire stone in the center of our gold rings "Co-" was not inscribed in front of "Big South Champions" in thick, capital letters. On one side the CSU helmet with a cutlass was inscribed. On the opposing was a black dot that read "EG21" in gold font.

After the ring ceremony we were likened to a bunch of 20-something girls who had just been proposed to, showing off our hardware to anyone who would be polite enough to let us brag. We were so busy with our ring fingers we almost missed the surprise ceremony that followed.

Ed Gadson had made his way back to CSU's campus for the banner and ring ceremony with his wife, Eddie's mom, Paula. Unbeknownst to us, they weren't here just for the banner and ring ceremonies, they had a gift for us. The Edward A. Gadson Memorial Scholarship Fund had been set up; they were here to shake the first recipient's hand and award him a scholarship. The player who received this esteemed honor would be a walk-on player who displayed heart and determination, just like Eddie.

Ed and Paula not only handed out the first scholarship, they helped to hand pick the first recipient. He was one of Eddie's best friends: Darius Jackson.

At the time this book went to print in the fall of 2015, the 2005 Buccaneers are the only football team to win a conference championship in school history. Better records have been posted and national rankings have been awarded, but no other team has earned a spot on the banner alongside the 2005 team. We gained wins as one unit, but many individuals were recognized for their outstanding performances. The conference offensive and defensive players of the year donned CSU cutlasses and we became the most highly decorated team in the conference that season.

The only awards listed are the Edward A. Gadson Memorial Scholarship winners from the past 10 years. Ten percent of the proceeds from book sales will go to the Edward A. Gadson Memorial Scholarship Fund at Charleston Southern University to support players like Eddie Gadson, Darius Jackson, and the ones listed on the following page. Each of these young men walked onto the football team at Charleston Southern and displayed some of the qualities that made Eddie Gadson such an inspiration.

To view individual conference accolades, go to http://BelieveEG21.com/awards

EDWARD A. GADSON
MEMORIAL SCHOLARSHIP WINNERS

2006: Darius Jackson
2007: Alex Thomas
2008: Matt Bach
2009: Austin Bloedoorn
2010: L.B. Cravey
2011: Zac Johnston

2012: Austin Wald
2013: Tre Deloach
2014: Tre Deloach
2015: Chris Nwanegwo and Stephen Cagle

10% of book proceeds will be donated to the Edward A. Gadson Memorial
Scholarship Fund. If you wish to make individual contributions
to the scholarship fund, go to http://BelieveEG21.com/scholarship

AFTERWORD

Coach Mills' staff varied each year, but he remained head coach of the Bucs for another seven seasons. Defensive coaches Perkins and Barrows left CSU to pursue head coaching careers. Darrell Perkins landed at the University of Maryland as the defensive backs coach and Steve Barrows is currently the head coach at Kentucky Christian University. Offensively, Chuck Kelly stayed with Mills through 2011 and now coaches the offensive line at Webber International.

Coach Mills retired from football after the 2012 season. He had accomplished many of his life's goals and left his mark on the Charleston Southern football program. Before he retired, he predicted that the upcoming senior class would have one of the best years in the program's history. He currently resides in Northern California where he is the Executive Pastor at Southwinds Church. Coach Jamey Chadwell, the receivers coach during the 2005 season, spent time at North Greenville University and Delta State University before returning "home" in 2013 as the Bucs new head coach. Coach Chadwell went 10-3 in his first season as head coach.

Though Ed and Paula Gadson are no longer married, they

remain good friends. They speak to each other multiple times each week and they were extremely helpful during the creation of this book. Ed stays current with CSU football and is frequently seen cheering in the stands wearing blue and gold. Each year the Gadsons are involved in the selection of the Edward A. Gadson Memorial Scholarship winner.

Nick Ellis was named to the All Academic Big South Team in 2006 and to the First Team Big South Conference Team in 2007, his senior year. Along the way he became CSU's all time points leader and was elected team captain after his senior season. Nick went into teaching and is currently the Assistant Principal at Ola High School in his hometown of McDonough, Georgia.

CJ Hirschman was selected to the Second Team Big South Conference Team in 2005 and the First Team Big South Conference Team in 2006. He also earned Second Team Big South honors for his duties as a punt returner in 2006. After graduating in three and a half years, according to our early graduation schemes, he moved to Charlotte, North Carolina and opened his own business.

Collin Drafts went on to become the mostly highly decorated player in Charleston Southern football history. He earned almost every quarterback record in the Charleston Southern and Big South record books with over 10,000 total yards and accounted for over 90 touchdowns as a four-year starter. He was named the Conference Player of the Year in 2005 and was later inducted into the CSU Athletic Hall of Fame. Today he coaches high school football in Florida with aspirations of becoming a head coach.

Okeba Rollinson never looked back once he earned his starting role. He was named Second Team Big South Conference in 2006 and again in 2007. Throughout his career he came up with big plays and even bigger hits when the team needed him. He finished his MBA in 2013 and is a quality assurance analyst in North Charleston, South Carolina.

As for me, I learned one of the most important lessons of my life on November 19, 2005. I spent weeks being bitter about my

To read Paula Gadson's full interview, go to http://BelieveEG21.com/paula

injury, something I saw as senseless that could have cost the team. But I wasn't supposed to be on the field. Okeba played a different style of game than me. He gambled more than me and the final play, when he knocked the ball down, was a huge bet. Had the quarterback pump faked and gone overhead, this story wouldn't be the same. But he was playing and I was watching. The 2005 championship season taught me that everything happens for a reason. My most important contribution to the season came 10 years later; in the form of a book. My broken thumb afforded me the opportunity to play a fifth season of football. Though I had already graduated, the same time as CJ, I began working on my MBA and cherished my last season of football. A season in which I was elected team captain, alongside the receiver Markus Murry, by my fellow teammates.

Ten years later the Bucs still have a tight bond. It is not uncommon to see photos of teammates grinning, arm in arm, at one another's weddings. We greet each other with hugs more often than handshakes. As Darius Jackson put it, "Even though we may not talk that often, we still have a bond. We come from different backgrounds but we spent more time with each other than we did with anyone else. We don't interact that much, but we pick up right where we left off when we see each other."

We continued our winning streak into 2006, when we won another nine straight games. Although 2005 was the only year we painted "EG21" on Buccaneer Field, we remained undefeated at home until October of 2007. Eddie Gadson's jersey was retired during the 2010 season. It was the first, and only, jersey retired for CSU football.

The feelings and the memories of the 2005 season will be forever ours. Rings will lose their luster and pictures will fade, but we will always be Champions. We will always believe.

To read Ed Gadson's full interview, go to http://BelieveEG21.com/edgadson

ACKNOWLEDGEMENTS

Before I wrote this book I never paid this section much attention. Now that I've gone through this process or journey or whatever you want to call it, I completely understand. Books, especially ones recreating real life events, are not something one person creates. This story required that I seek help from a number of people.

First off, I want to thank God for giving me the ability to communicate through my writing. I've known for a long time what effect books can have on people, I just never thought I'd be the one doing the storytelling. Thank you, God, for putting this story on my heart to share with the world. I am merely a medium through which He has worked.

I want to thank each person on this list with sincerity. You've helped me accomplish something on my bucket list and I'm forever grateful for your support.

Starting with the beginning of life, I want to thank my parents. Momma for inspiring me to write this book and always believing in me, even when I was jobless and out of my mind. Dad for teaching me the game that has lead to so many positive experiences in my life and has literally taken me around the world in the process. Aunt Stephanie for being my editor and dealing with my sub-par early drafts that were incoherent, rambling, and filled with football jargon. I couldn't have pulled this story together without you! And thank you Katie for all of your love, support, and encouragement through this process. You mean the world to me.

Thank you coaches. Thank you Coach Kevin Brown for showing me how to play with passion and how to read the guards. Thank you Coach Jay Mills for offering me a scholarship; you changed my life. Also, thank you for providing extensive notes about this time period. Without your attention to detail, this story would have lacked a number of key facts. Thank you Coach Darrell Perkins for believing in me as a young man and giving me the confidence to stand out and make a difference. Thank you Toby Harkins, even though you're not a coach, for never letting me get complacent and telling me I should be the one to set the example. Also for helping heal my broken body for all those years. Thank you to every one of my coaches (listed and not) for pushing me. I didn't like any of you all the time, but I needed all of you all the time. Whether you intended to or not, you helped shape me into the man writing these words today.

Thank you teammates. Thank you Sheldon Evans for taking me under your wing by giving me guidance and someone to look up to. Thank you Josh Warrior for always pushing me to be a better man and football player. Thank you Marvin McHellon for showing me how to give everything and for being an example to so many of us when we needed an older brother. Thank you Jeff Crisp, Anthony "Moe" Moore, Ryan "Reggie" Robertson, and Collin Drafts for showing me a good time on my recruiting trip. Coming to CSU was the best decision of my life and I'm thankful we're still part of each others' lives. Special thanks to Collin for allowing me to interview you, reviewing an early draft, and for being such an integral part of this process. I appreciate our friendship and our football talks, I hope they (both) continue for a long time. Thank you CJ Hirschman for not only your support during the writing process, but your friendship for all these years.

Thank you everyone who helped me produce this work. Thank you Dr. Jairy C. Hunter for giving me the school's blessing to print this story. Thank you Tam Odom for sharing your photos. Thank you John Strubel for guiding me through this process and helping me improve my writing. Thank you Nate Winkler, Alan Spears, and Paul Chelmis of SOUTH for all of the design work that went into making this book first class. Thank you Kevin O'Rourke for compiling the information from CSU athletics to help me reconstruct this story and for your time reviewing an early draft.

Thank you interviewees/coaches/teammates. Thank you Nick Ellis, Coach Barrows, Reggie Robertson, Darius Jackson, Coach Chadwell, Jim O'Connor, Okeba Rollinson, and Markus Murry for allowing me to interrupt your lives to talk about this story. I truly enjoyed our talks and hearing your stories.

Last, and most important, thank you Ed and Paula Gadson. I could not, and would not, have done this without your support. Thank you for letting me probe into the darkest time in your lives. Thank you for sharing everything you shared. Thank you for your support, it means so much to me that you'd allow me to tell a portion of Eddie's story. People ask me what I enjoyed most about this process and my answer is how much better I got to know Eddie. Your son blessed a lot of people during his time here on Earth. Thank you for sharing him with the world and especially with the CSU football team.

Thank you to my audience who has followed the production of *Believe EG21*. Your encouragement through this process kept me going more times than you know. Thank you all for helping me to "write the book I've always wanted to read."

READER'S GUIDE

BELIEVE EG21 BY MIKE MCCANN

For Discussion:

1.) Reading the lessons learned from a football player's perspective, how do sports help prepare young people for the challenges they'll face later in life?

2.) The author implies divine intervention had something to do with the outcome of the Coastal Carolina game. Do you believe God or Eddie helped Charleston Southern during that game? If so, why?

3.) The fact that football is a dangerous sport is widely known and discussed. Are the tradeoffs of playing sports (i.e. life lessons of discipline, hard work, etc.) worth the risk of physical injury?

4.) The National Collegiate Athletic Association (NCAA) does not allow colleges and universities to pay its student-athletes. Do you think the hours student-athletes spend playing collegiate athletics justifies payment from their respective schools? Why or why not?

5.) Six players were removed from the team days before a "must-win" game against Gardner Webb for failing a drug test. Do you agree with Coach Mills' decision to dismiss the players or should he have handled the matter internally by punishing them with playing time and extra running? At what cost would you be willing to preserve the character of your own team if you were in Coach Mills' shoes?

6.) The Gadson family had no obligation to spend time with the Charleston Southern football team after their son's death, yet they continued coming to games and supporting the team. Why do you think they continued to stay involved with the team?

7.) "EG21" was painted on the field during each home game for Charleston Southern. In what ways do we hold on to lost loved ones after they've passed as the team did?

8.) Coach Mills and his coaching staff were influential to the players' growth into young adulthood. Why was their influence so heavy in the players' lives? Who has been influential in your life the way the coaches were for the Charleston Southern football team?

9.) Young men of all backgrounds, races, and income levels were a part of this and every college football team in America. Young men who more than likely would not have crossed paths under other circumstances. What other activities besides sports brings people of all backgrounds together like we've seen in *Believe EG21* to achieve a common goal? How can we, as a country, encourage more of these types of behavior?

For more information about the book or the author,
go to www.BelieveEG21.com.

Or follow us on social media:
Facebook.com/BelieveEG21
Twitter.com/EG21Believe
Instagram.com/BelieveEG21

Made in the USA
Charleston, SC
10 February 2016